EMPLOYABILITY
IN A
HIGH PERFORMANCE
ECONOMY

EMPLOYABILITY
IN A
HIGH PERFORMANCE
ECONOMY

BARRY G. SHECKLEY
LOIS LAMDIN
MORRIS T. KEETON

cael
The Council for Adult & Experiential Learning
Chicago

ISBN: 0-9628073-3-8

cael
The Council for Adult & Experiential Learning
223 West Jackson Boulevard, Suite 510
Chicago, Illinois 60606

Editorial, Design & Production Services by Winthrop Publishing Company, Waynesville, North Carolina

Manufactured in the United States of America

CONTENTS

Acknowledgments   **xi**

Foreword   **xv**

PART 1
Employability: A New Goal   **1**

Chapter 1: The Value of Employability   3

What Is Employability?   4

Employability, Competitiveness, & the High
Performance Enterprise   5

A Win-Win Scenario   8

A New Infrastructure   8

Chapter 2: Secure Workers, Competitive Companies   11

Why the Change in Competitiveness & Job Security?   11

Collective Bargaining with Lost Markets & Jobs   13

Competing Worldwide the Old Way   14

Toward a New Strategy of Global Competition   16

A New Strategy in Education & Training   17

A Government Framework for Competitiveness
& Employability   20

PART 2
Partnerships for Employability: A Win-Win Scenario   23

Chapter 3: Two Approaches to Employability Education   25

Employee Growth & Development Programs   25

Work Settings as Learning Environments   27

Building Win-Win Partnerships   30

Chapter 4: Employers as Partners   31

Why Participate?   31

How to Get the Benefits   31

    Situation 1: Declining Productivity, Rising Competition   32

    Situation 2: Rapid Turnover, Hot Competition   33

    Situation 3: Collective Bargaining & Downsizing while Adding New Subsidiaries   34

    Situation 4: Small Businesses with Tight Margins   36

Getting the Added Benefits   39

What If an Employer Is Committed to Cheap Labor?   40

Specific Costs of Employability Programs   42

Training as an Overall Business Strategy   44

    Live Case Studies   46

Learning Organizations & Total Quality Management   46

Chapter 5: Workers & Unions as Partners   49

How the Worker Benefits   49

The Employee Growth & Development Program   51

    Costs & Risks to the Worker   54

    An Important Role for College Studies   55

Learning in Work Settings   55

What Employability Means to Unions   57

The Union as Advocate & Guarantor of Employability   58

Chapter 6: Education Providers as Partners   61

Are All These Providers Essential?   63

The Role of the Public Schools   66

A New Role for Colleges & Universities   68

Barriers to Cooperation   69

Slow Response Time   70

Inflexibility   71

Inappropriate Teaching Methods   71

Inappropriate Content   71

Lack of Timely Decisions   72

Resistance to Change   72

Unfamiliarity with Adult Students   73

Limited Range of Services   73

Rewards of Cooperation   75

Requirements for Schools' Successful Participation   75

What Schools Can Gain from Participating   79

Chapter 7: The Federal & State Governments as Partners   83

How the States & the Nation Benefit   84

The Context for National Gains   85

Actions to Undo   88

Actions to Take   92

Incentives for Employed Workers   92

Incentives for Unemployed Workers   94

Setting an Example   96

Building Blocks of a Nationwide Employability Program   98

PART 3
Upgrading the Workforce   103

Chapter 8: The Skills Employers Seek & Employees Need   105

Lifelong Learning as a Reality   106

What Employers Say They Want   107

What Employees Say They Want   108

A Consensus on Necessary Skills   109

Knowing How to Learn   111

Basic Academic Skills: Reading, Writing, & Computation 111

Communications 112

Cognitive Skills 112

Personal & Career Development Skills 113

Interpersonal Skills & Effectiveness in Groups 113

Organizational Effectiveness & Leadership 113

Transferability of Workplace Skills 114

Employability Skills as Cognitive Processing 115

Chapter 9: Closing the Skills Gap 119

Five Transitions 120

From High School to Work 121

From College to Work 124

From Work Back to School 125

From Welfare to School & Work 127

Work as School 128

The Choice of Learning Arenas 129

Closing the Skills Gap: Scale of Effort & Focus of Effort 130

Scale of Effort 130

Focus of Effort 131

Credentialing 132

Problems with the Current System 132

Toward a National Credentialing System 134

Benefits of Skills Credentialing 136

Searching for a Job 138

Chapter 10: Avoiding a Two-Tiered Society 141

Catch-22: The Compounding Circle of Disadvantage 141

Race 142

Gender 142

Previous Education & Training 142

Native Language 144

Years of Work Experience 144

The Scope of the Problem of Disadvantaged Workers   145

Overcoming the Pattern of Disadvantage   146

   Public Schooling   148

   Employer-Sponsored Training   148

   Private-Sector Initiatives   148

   Government Incentives   149

   Coping with Multiple Barriers   150

An Attitude Toward Disadvantage   151

PART 4
Pulling It All Together   153

Chapter 11: The Principles of Effective Employability Programs   155

Principle 1: Give Learner-Workers Choices   156

   Worker Contributions to Employability Programs   158

   A Profile of the New Learner-Workers   158

Principle 2: Provide Learner-Workers the Tools They Need to Make Informed Choices   159

Principle 3: Ensure Advocacy by All Partners   162

Principle 4: Provide Access for Everyone   163

Principle 5: Engage in Proactive Outreach   163

Principle 6: Provide Prepaid Tuition   165

Principle 7: Remove Institutional Barriers & Disincentives   166

Principle 8: Start Prior Learning Assessment Programs   168

Principle 9: Provide Workplace Support Systems   169

Principle 10: Establish & Maintain Goals & Values   170

Using the Principles in Practice   171

Chapter 12: Work Settings as Learning Environments   173

Developing Skills on the Job   173

Supervisors as Instructors   175

The Role of Classroom Programs   177

   The Continuum of Competence   179

   Limitations of Classroom Training   181

Achieving High Performance   182

Partnership Roles   185

Chapter 13: Toward a National Policy   189

A Vision of Near-Universal Employability   190

Public Policy   191

Defining Employability   194

Effects on Human Resource Development   195

Financing a Nationwide Employability Program   196

Coordinating Partner Efforts & Incentives for Cooperation   200

Appendix: What Is CAEL?   203

Bibliography   207

Index   215

About the Authors   231

Figure List   235

ACKNOWLEDGMENTS

This book grew out of the experience of the Council for Adult and Experiential Learning (CAEL) in codesigning and managing employee growth and development programs (EGDPs) with diverse corporations and unions. Workers' participation in formal study grew to levels unmatched before. Their successes and struggles raised new questions on ways to enhance worker morale, increase their productivity, reduce turnover, and cope with changing job requirements. Unions have come to see their tasks in a new light and to find new ways they can serve their members. New ways to respond to learner needs — even those of younger, non-working learners — have emerged for education providers through their experience with participants in the CAEL joint ventures, as these EGDPs have been called. It is to this experience and to the many players in the CAEL joint ventures that the authors owe their greatest debt.

Among those at CAEL, first mention must go to Pamela Tate, now president of CAEL, who was the senior consultant for the UAW/Ford National Development and Training Center (NDTC) in developing its College and University Options Program (CUOP), the first of the CAEL joint ventures. But for her pioneering, the entire employability effort here reported might never have occurred. The staff of this and later EGDPs have also provided crucial insights into the potential and the problems of EGDPs. We make particular mention of Elinor Greenberg, head of the PATHWAYS to the Future Program for some five initial years;

Mary Fugate, who reviewed the text from the perspective of an experienced CAEL practitioner; and both Diana Bamford-Rees and Laura Winters, who played major administrative roles throughout the early joint ventures.

Across the table, with final say in the design and conduct of these early employability programs, were the corporate and labor leaders with whom CAEL worked. Helping also with the critique of this manuscript have been Hugh Walsh of the Communications Workers of America and Dorothy Shields, education director of the AFL-CIO and a member of the CAEL Board of Trustees. Gerard Voit, earlier with Bell of Pennsylvania and for a time a senior consultant to CAEL, read major portions of the manuscript and responded. Corporate leaders on the CAEL Board of Trustees — notably Fred Cook of Mountain Bell Telephone and Badi Foster of Aetna — and the board as a whole since 1984 have contributed specific ideas and seasoned counsel and perspective.

A major event along the way toward this book's writing was the 1989 Little Rock conference, *Toward a More Productive Work Force*. It was initiated by the Commission on Higher Education and the Adult Learner of the American Council on Education (1980 - 89). The conference, hosted by then Governor Clinton, was cosponsored by the National Governors' Association (NGA), the American Council on Education (ACE), the College Board, and CAEL. Evelyn Ganzglass of the NGA, Henry Spille of ACE, Carol Aslanian and Elena Morris of the College Board, and Morris Keeton of CAEL were the principal planners. Its papers are drawn upon in these pages. It was made possible by a key grant by the John D. and Catherine T. MacArthur Foundation.

The authors have drawn upon others' work for our picture of the emerging global economy and its impact on American competitiveness, the American job market, and strategies for economic recovery. Our work builds on theirs, not duplicating nor second-guessing them. Notable among them are Ira Magaziner and colleagues in their work *America's Choice*, and Anthony

Carnevale and his colleagues of the American Society for Training and Development and the U.S. Department of Labor.

The authors are greatly indebted to institutions for which they have worked or now work and to colleagues in those institutions. For Lois Lamdin these include Carnegie-Mellon University, Hostos Community College (CUNY), Empire State College and CLEO, a consortium of 34 colleges and universities, and the Business Development and Training Center of Great Valley (PA). For Barry Sheckley they include the University of Connecticut's School of Education and particularly Professor George Allen, and from the Research Center for Organizational Learning, colleagues Barry Goff and Sandra Hastings. Larry Fox, deputy commissioner of labor in Connecticut, has reviewed much of the manuscript and provided comments enabling us to make significant revisions. For Morris Keeton the collegial help came from his years with Antioch College (1947-77), and CAEL (1977-89), and most recently (1990 - present) with the University of Maryland University College.

The authors warmly appreciate help given by foundations. In addition to the MacArthur Foundation support, the W. K. Kellogg Foundation rounded out some 13 years of financial support for CAEL, beginning in 1977, with a grant to CAEL in early 1990 to support Morris Keeton's work on this book and to facilitate the work with states that is briefly reported in Chapter 7. The Ford Foundation, with particular interest in the hourly workforce and its ethnically diverse and relatively disadvantaged subpopulations, provided complementary support.

As always with so complex an undertaking, professional and support staff have played a significant role in the completion of this book. Standing out among them are Lynn Schroeder of Winthrop Marketing, who coordinated all of the editing, design, promotion and production of the book; Judith Gallagher, our developmental editor; India Koopman, our copy editor; and Gerlinde Keeton Young, Morris Keeton's administrative assistant.

Our families have managed handsomely the challenge of

encouraging us, sustaining us when energies flagged and spirits drooped, and avoiding the appearance that we were neglecting or abusing them in our preoccupation with work. We salute them.

The authors divided the labor of making first drafts. All three subsequently reworked the entire manuscript so that no one of us can claim any part as his or hers alone. We rather like the result.

We regret that practicalities require us to stop work now, before we learn more and can try longer to get the story right. Although our standing motto is the widely publicized "Learning Never Ends," we have finally had to acknowledge that, for this project, learning ends now. We do not promise, however, that we will not appear with second and third thoughts later.

The authors hereby make the usual plea that our sponsors and home institutions are not responsible for our own errors of omission or commission. Finally, we acknowledge that the utility of this work will turn entirely upon the astuteness of our readers and their willingness and effectiveness in applying the ideas stimulated by this work to their own day-to-day tasks. Without this collaboration, our work will have been in vain.

— Barry G. Sheckley, Lois Lamdin, Morris T. Keeton
August 1993

FOREWORD

Employability — a single word that embraces the goal of all of the current talk about workforce education and training, that holds the key to how this country can build a workforce able to compete globally.

For years, the most vexing question asked of those of us who are concerned with providing training to enable individual workers to retain their jobs or be eligible for new ones in an evolving economy has been, *Just what do you intend to train them for?*

Of course, we have had answers. We have said that employers must look ahead and tell us what their needs will be in five, 10 or more years so that workers can learn the requisite skills. We have said that schools must get better at teaching basic communication skills. We have said that workers should be language, math, and computer literate. We have said that workers must *learn how to learn* so that they can keep up with changing technologies.

We have said, and meant, all of that, and we were right. But our answers were both too limited and too vague, and they did not convince enough people to expend enough resources to enable enough working people to survive and compete in what has become an increasingly risky job market. Now, with the addition of the *concept of employability* — not only to our vocabularies but to our thinking about workforce training — we can work with specific objectives that apply to *all* workforce training, whether in schools or colleges, on the job or in employer- or union-sponsored courses and workshops, by collaborative or individual efforts.

What we want to do, what we *must* do, is ensure that every person currently in the workforce or approaching working age has access to the resources to achieve employability on his or her own terms. That is, all must have not only the skills and competencies to fulfill the needs of their present jobs but the ability, flexibility, and means to learn new skills and competencies as required — as well as the will to do so. The work ethic is also relevant here and can be incorporated into learning objectives.

If you look at the lists of competencies generated by today's employers and others concerned with workforce training, you will find that they are very similar to what educators have long expounded as the broad goals of education. To become and remain employable, men and women must have the ability to use all the various languages — technical, mathematical, and linguistic — through which we communicate and do our work. They must have the ability to work well with each other, to communicate and cooperate. They must have learned how to approach and solve problems, to apply the information they already have in new situations. They must have, above all, the ability — and the desire — to learn, so that when their job requirements change, when new technologies are introduced, when their current jobs disappear and they must seek different kinds of employment, they are empowered to do so.

The authors of *Employability in a High Performance Economy* claim that this country can achieve near universal employability. By this they do *not* mean that no one will ever again be unemployed. They *do* mean that all members of the current or prospective workforce can achieve those broad, generic skills that will enable them to survive change, adapt to new work demands, and continue learning. They *do* mean that workers will be eligible for a broader range of existing jobs and able to adapt to innovation with a greater degree of confidence.

The authors do not minimize the effort such an achievement will take, both from the individual worker and from the society that must provide the resources to make it possible. But they explain how a series of collaborative partnerships among government, schools, business, labor, and individuals can be created that will get the job done. They also delineate the costs and benefits accruing to each sector, as well as the legislative and tax disincentives that are impeding current efforts.

The models for such partnerships already exist in workforce education programs administered by the Council for Adult and Experiential Learning (CAEL) and in many other private and public initiatives across the United States. Moreover, as national concern increases about how to move those who are currently unemployed into work rebuilding America's infrastructure and how to retrain vast numbers of displaced military and defense-industry personnel for peacetime work, the concept of employability takes on special urgency.

Thanks to the efforts of such groups as the Commission on the Skills of the American Workforce, the American Society for Training and Development, the Secretary of Labor's Commission on Achieving Necessary Skills, and other farsighted national efforts, a new school agenda is in the process of being formed. The emphasis of the 1992 presidential and congressional campaigns and the interest of other politicians across the country in training suggest that the political will is growing to become proactive in efforts to build a competent, confident American workforce by investing in the training of both young people and adults.

Employability in a High Performance Economy also suggests that not all of the new worker learning must, or should, come from formal training and education. New insights on the power of the worksite as a learning environment indicate that much more can be done to structure and encourage learning in factories, offices, shops, and laboratories — and to make certain that such learning is formally recognized in some nationally accepted currency of credit or record of competency achievement.

This book challenges all of us — whether we are teachers or legislators, corporate or union leaders, professional, service, or technical workers — to take an active part in building the work-force that will create the economy of the twenty-first century.

— Pamela Tate
President, Council for Adult and Experiential Learning

1

EMPLOYABILITY: A NEW GOAL

PART 1

addresses the major themes of the book — the value of employability, the new meaning of competitiveness in a global economy,
and the importance of partnerships among industry, workers and
unions, education providers, and government in achieving a
better trained, more productive workforce.

Chapter 1

defines employability through the examples of three workers. It
explains why a widely employable workforce is critical to competitiveness and why employability must occur in the context of
an increasing array of high-performance enterprises.

Chapter 2

discusses how a new agenda of concerns arises from the dynamic
of employability, productivity, and competitiveness in the 1990s
and how this agenda differs from that which preoccupied employers, unions, education providers, and government prior to the
1970s. This chapter points to the new role of learning in American
society and makes the case for businesses to become learning as
well as producing organizations.

1.

THE VALUE OF EMPLOYABILITY

John, Jules, and Joan worked for a U.S. communications company manufacturing internationally distributed components for facsimile (fax) machines. Each had been earning just over $16 per hour. The company had a good benefits program, including a strong pension plan for which they were eligible within five years. Without warning, the company installed a new automated system that eliminated 70 percent of the jobs on the production line. John, Jules, and Joan were all given notice.

John had been a hard worker, loyal to the company and conscientious about the quality of his work, but his skills were limited. This was his first job, and all he knew about electronics was what he had learned in a narrowly defined job with no opportunities to develop new skills or broaden his base of experience. After being laid off, John spent 18 months looking for a job similar to his old one. But in his area of the country the electronics industry was either downsizing its manufacturing capacity or automating. There were simply no jobs available. John finally got a job at $6 per hour as a gardener's assistant. He had to sell his house and radically change his and his family's lifestyle. Since he lost his pension benefits, he is now uncertain about his own long-term future and about his ability to help his children attend college.

The merchants in John's town will feel the pinch as John and former co-workers spend less on food, clothing, and services.

The state and the country will feel the pinch because people like John will pay fewer taxes. And, in an era when the United States needs more skilled workers than are available, a group of potentially valuable members of the workforce — John and his peers — are effectively sidelined.

Jules and Joan fared somewhat better. A few years earlier, Jules had taken courses in electronics theory and computer-assisted design (CAD) at a local community college. Joan had also expanded her skills, not through college but through her work in an experimental cellular manufacturing unit within the company. The company had encouraged cross-training within cellular work teams, and Joan had responded. As a result, she developed a wide variety of skills in set-up procedures, assembly processes, and inventory control. Joan also expanded her knowledge about manufacturing processes during team discussions about how parts could be redesigned to reduce production time.

Once laid off, both Jules and Joan were able to obtain employment. Jules is now an assistant in the component design department of the same company and Joan has joined a nearby company. Although both are earning less, each will shortly be in line for a wage increase that will more than make up the difference. Most important, neither they nor their families had to undergo wrenching changes in their lifestyles.

WHAT IS EMPLOYABILITY?

Jules and Joan have achieved *employability*. They have broadened their skills, thereby increasing their flexibility as to the kinds of work they can do. Even if Jules had been unable to get another job in the same company, chances are he would soon have gotten work elsewhere.

Employability, or employment security, means being qualified for currently available work, whether with a present employer or elsewhere. It means maintaining essential knowledge and competence in a present job while gaining new knowledge and competence that will keep the worker employable as job requirements change.

Notice that we did not trumpet Jules' and Joan's *job security*. *Job security* means simply that rules and regulations are in place to ensure that a worker will always have a job within a given company. Job security may be an undesirable goal for the U.S. economy since it fosters a static workforce. Employability, on the other hand, provides the dynamic workforce required for today's global economy.

Maintaining an employable workforce means developing individuals who have basic verbal and numeric literacy, the inter-personal skills to work well in teams, the flexibility to take change in stride, the cognitive skills to analyze and synthesize ideas, the initiative to solve problems and, above all, the motivation and ability to learn. No matter what technological, political, or structural changes occur in the emerging world economy and our own, individuals who are in this sense employable will always have an edge in finding productive, remunerative work. Employable workers will always hold a competitive edge in the workforce over those who have focused on job security.

Employability of a growing proportion of the workforce is a practical option for any developed industrial economy. To date, social policy in the United States has failed to provide the option of employability for all who are capable of productive work. But achieving employability of more than 95 percent of the workforce is feasible. To see what is involved, let us revisit Jules and Joan.

EMPLOYABILITY, COMPETITIVENESS, & THE HIGH PERFORMANCE ENTERPRISE

Within a year after John, Jules, and Joan were laid off, Joan received a further shock when her second company went out of business. Its strategy for competing had been to standardize and automate to the fullest extent possible, deskilling all possible jobs, thereby keeping payroll and costs per unit of production low. The firm continued to lose business, however, because a few competitors, while also using state-of-the-art equipment for automation, had built worker teams capable of using the equipment to customize jobs and enhance client services. With more highly skilled workers, they were able to offer a better product and service than Joan's company could offer.

This example illustrates the dynamic partnership required for improving American productivity and maintaining employment options for American workers. Workers who develop their employability must be complemented by companies that improve their competitiveness enough to sustain their businesses. For companies in today's world market, this means becoming increasingly high performance enterprises (Dertouzos, Lester, and Solow 1989) that achieve a winning combination of price and quality of services and products. This winning combination requires what for most U.S. businesses will be a fundamental change in their approach to productivity.

A June 1990 report by the National Center on Education and the Economy (NCEE) disclosed that most American employers, like Jules' employer and like employers in other industrialized nations, have sought competitiveness by investing heavily in automation, computerization, and other modes of technological change in order to deskill their workforces and hold down the cost of labor. Not surprisingly, few employers who used this automation strategy in 1990 reported a disparity between the skills of their workers and the demands of their jobs.

> *The organization of America's workplaces today is largely modeled after the system of mass manufacture pioneered during the early 1900s. The premise is simple: Break complex jobs into a myriad of simple rote tasks, which the worker then repeats with machine-like efficiency. The system is managed by a*

small group of educated planners and supervisors who do the thinking for the organization.

But in the world's best companies, new high performance work organizations are replacing this "Taylor" method ... The new high performance forms of work organization ... require large investments in training.

Workers' pay levels often rise to reflect their greater qualifications and responsibilities. But the productivity and quality gains more than offset the costs to the company of the higher wages and skills development.

Despite these advantages, 95 percent of American companies still cling to the old forms of work organization (NCEE 1990, 203).

It is highly unlikely that the Taylor approach to productivity (automating and deskilling) can sustain the competitiveness of any country's enterprises in the emerging world economy, especially not that of the United States, with its high wage base and cost of living. To sustain or enhance their competitiveness, most U.S. businesses will have to transform their current modes of operation to the new high performance mode, developing managers to a point where they make the worksite itself a productive learning environment, similar to that which Joan experienced.

The disparate, even adversarial, relationships that exist today among workers, unions, employers, and government agencies cannot sustain America as a leader in the new world economy. To develop high performance enterprises, workers and employers must engage in a dynamic, cooperative partnership that is supplemented by supporting alliances among unions, government, and education providers.

The sustained employability of all workers will, we believe, depend on the ability of these partnerships to cultivate work settings that support the continual improvement of business practices by encouraging the growth and development of individual workers.

A WIN-WIN SCENARIO

Our message in this book is that all involved — employers, employees, unions, and governments — can gain critical advantages from cooperating to increase the employability of the workforce.

We propose a set of guiding objectives and principles for implementing the necessary partnerships among business and labor, state and federal governments, and providers of education and training at all levels. We will use examples to illustrate specifically how to apply these objectives and principles, revealing both what is feasible and how complex implementation will be.

John, Jules, and Joan are not expendable. They cannot be relegated to the status of statistics, victims of change, forgotten except by their social workers and the postal workers who deliver their welfare checks. They and millions like them must be integrated into the new workforce that America has to develop if it is to remain competitive on the world stage. Employability is a goal for each and every worker, but it is also the way for American business and industry to maintain strength and leadership in the decades to come.

A NEW INFRASTRUCTURE

To achieve both employability and competitiveness, the United States will have to create a new infrastructure of policies and institutional arrangements. Why? For four reasons. First, no one group of the essential partners — not business alone, not federal or state government alone, and not unions or education providers alone — can generate and sustain an employable, optimally productive workforce. All of the partners are needed, as we show in the next chapters, and their contributions must be effectively orchestrated.

Second, a new infrastructure is needed because the mere existence of policies, even with shared goodwill and the desire to cooperate, will not ensure that the policies are made to work. Also required are incentives that make it attractive to adhere to the policies. Procedures and institutions to monitor progress, adjust incentives, facilitate adaptation to major changes in the economic and social environment, and, possibly, enforce fair play among the partners are needed as well.

The third reason for a new infrastructure is that the United States has witnessed an enormous proliferation of education providers in the years since World War II. Their rise and survival signals a great diversity of training and education needs within the society; their continued prosperity shows that many niches for successful educational institutions and service providers continue to exist. At the same time (perhaps contributing to the explosion of providers), the problem of verbal and numeric illiteracy has persisted, and public outcry against the inadequate performance of the schools has grown.

The authors have sought a nonpartisan overview of this network of providers, have explained the advantages and difficulties of providing learning opportunities through such a decentralized and differentiated system of providers, and have developed a vision of how this "nonsystem" may need to evolve in response to the needs of the economy and society. In the past two years, the movement toward European economic union has seen the emergence of near unanimity among its prospective partners that their educational systems must be integrated for optimal economic success. As this concept moves to implementation, the American educational enterprise will have a new rival in the world market — which should spur it on to greater creativity in its use of resources.

A fourth factor arguing for a new infrastructure is central to discussions of the United States and similar economies. While the layoffs we refer to have been commonplace since 1978 in different industries, the total number of jobs filled has grown steadily since then. It grew at a rate of 2.3 million jobs per year in the 1970s. Recently the rate has slowed, but 1.5 million new jobs per year are still expected in the 1990s (Carnevale 1991). A full grasp of the problem and the opportunity requires an understanding of this dynamic that eliminates jobs in some sectors while generating more jobs in other sectors.

While this pattern might give way to net losses in the depth of recession, such losses are unlikely to persist for long. A 95 percent or higher level of employability requires continual retraining of portions of the workforce for new lines of work. The policy-making apparatus of the society and its implementing institutions must be competent and flexible enough to adjust to changes as they occur.

To recap, we need a new infrastructure of policies and institutions for four reasons:

1. No one kind of partner alone can do the job;

2. Once the policies are in place, we need a way to make them work;

3. The field of education providers keeps changing; and

4. The workforce will require constant retraining as some categories of enterprise fail and others replace them.

Before addressing the makeup of the new infrastructure, we will discuss the essential partners who must function within it, their contributions, and the benefits they can derive from participation.

SECURE WORKERS, COMPETITIVE COMPANIES

The world is moving from a set of loosely linked economies to a closely intertwined world economy, from being dominated by a cold war between two great powers to increasingly decentralized political power. It is also moving from a time when learning was perceived as centered in formal education to a time when learning is understood to occur overwhelmingly in the workplace, the home, and the community. These changes upset many long-held assumptions about competitiveness, job security, the education and training of the workforce, and the government's role and responsibilities.

WHY THE CHANGE IN COMPETITIVENESS & JOB SECURITY?

Immediately after World War II, American industry had a large enough domestic economy to support it. Industry in other countries, such as Japan and Germany, was obliged to adapt to smaller markets with more diverse customers and to do so with fewer, less qualified workers. As a result, producers in those economies focused on flexibility, greater responsiveness to customer wants and needs, attention to quality of products and services, and greater investment in use of their human capital (Carnevale 1991, 12-14). These adjustments served those economies well, in due time, in outperforming American enterprise. American industry's lack of responsiveness to new market demands and its reluctance to correct ineffective management practices combined to change radically the job security of American workers, as well as the profitability of American business.

The changes were first evident on a large scale in the steel and automotive industries. In the automotive industry, for example, the 1978-82 layoffs reached the level of 50 percent of hourly employees. Temporary layoffs had occurred in the past, but these were permanent. The immediate cause of the layoffs was competition: a heavy loss of car sales to German, Japanese, and other foreign producers.

The second cause of diminished job security can be traced to new technologies. Prior to the 1980s, "Ma Bell" had provided assurances of job security similar to those in the automotive industry. The image of the loyal, protective matriarch was consonant with telecommunications workers' assumption that once employed by the telephone company, they were set for life. After the divestiture of AT&T, the interplay of corporate reorganization with technological changes made possible more production with fewer workers. It was no longer feasible for telecommunications employers to guarantee job security (Ferman, Hoyman, Cutcher-Gershenfeld, and Savoie 1991, 32-35). No one had envisioned a new digital recording technology that would make redundant half of the employees (mostly women) who answered information calls. No one dreamed that telephone installation could become a simple, do-it-yourself project, eliminating the jobs of thousands of skilled phone installers. The job losses were blamed in part on outside competition. But why was that competition so successful? First, U.S. wage levels were generally higher than those elsewhere. Second, our responsiveness to market interests was lower than our competitors'. Most importantly, our management was in many instances overstaffed and unable to sustain a level of productivity that could support high wages (Dertouzos, Lester, and Solow 1989).

Given the power of the combined forces of new technologies, increased global competition, and marginal management effectiveness, job security has become obsolete. Not even better management and newer patterns of customer service can reinstate it. If, for whatever causes, neither company nor union can ensure permanent jobs for those who are punctual, do their jobs well, and retrain on company time when changes occur, then what can they promise workers? Not job security, but the opportunity to stay employable whatever the changes of job demands and of work opportunities. This emphasis on employability is necessary because it has become impossible to promise job security on a one-employer-to-every-employee basis.

COLLECTIVE BARGAINING WITH LOST MARKETS & JOBS

The commitment to comprehensive development of workers at all levels is a relatively new phenomenon in American business. *"Throughout most of the history of labor-management relations in the United States, training and employee development played at best a minor role in collective bargaining"* (Ferman, et al 1991, 55). Among the first companies to make this new type of commitment to comprehensive worker development were the Big Three automakers. Their employee growth and development programs (EGDPs), which got fully underway in 1984-85, were followed within three years by similar ones in telecommunications, most notably within US WEST Communications, and later between AT&T, Bell of Pennsylvania, and a group of Ameritech companies and their unions, the Communications Workers of America (CWA) and International Brotherhood of Electrical Workers (IBEW).

While Ferman and colleagues identified some 204 corporations listed with the Department of Labor in 1978 as having joint labor- and management-sponsored training and employee development programs, none at that time had the inclusiveness of the 1984 and later auto and telecommunications EGDPs. Since 1984, the Council for Adult and Experiential Learning (CAEL) has assisted as co-designer, broker, and orchestrator of EGDP services for some 30 corporations, most of which provided the services as a result of bargaining with their respective unions.

Ford Motor Company's first EGDP was funded by agreement with United Auto Workers to set aside a nickel for every hour of hourly workers' regular shifts, plus 50 cents for every overtime hour. For a workforce of about 114,000 hourly employees in early 1984, this amounted to more than $1 million per month. In the 1984 round of collective bargaining, the "nickel fund" was increased to a dime to cover existing benefits, with additional funds provided for services such as retirement planning and substance abuse counseling.

In the case of another large employer and its unions, the initial agreement funded a three-year program for some 28,000 employees at $7.8 million. Three years later, the partners expanded the program from seven states to 14 and the eligible workforce to 40,000. More than $14 million was allocated to the program.

The shift from a policy of training only for immediately needed job skills to education and training for ongoing employability was not made out of charitable impulses, as both business and labor will testify. The shift was an integral part of a new strategy for effective competition.

COMPETING WORLDWIDE THE OLD WAY

In the past, a corporation gained stability and profitability by becoming one of the best in a particular line of business within its home country, establishing a reputation for value, and sustaining its share of the market for that set of products or services.

The ABC Engineering Company typified this strategy. In the early 1960s, a group of enterprising engineers incorporated to develop business applications for scientific technologies. They noticed one industry still dominated by the handcrafting techniques that had persisted for centuries. The founders of ABC combined a computer-based design system with the use of advanced plastics and adhesive materials to make the handcrafted process faster, more efficient, and more profitable.

Within a few short years, ABC's products dominated the market. By the end of the 1970s, virtually every shop in the United States that used this craft abandoned handmade methods, purchased ABC machines, and used ABC products. ABC's eminence peaked in the early 1980s, then began to erode. As the 1990s arrived, the company was wrestling with over 50 competitors for advantage in the market it had created.

ABC's problem — how to sustain competitive advantage — confronts many U.S. business enterprises. Traditionally, firms faced with competitors have fought for advantage by using cost controls to keep prices down. They drop products or services, add others, lay off workers, and reach out to find enough markets to keep unit costs down and prices competitive. Today this strategy limits a company (NCEE 1990). Competitors from abroad can beat American businesses that focus on deskilling, in part because of their lower labor costs and at times because of unfavorable exchange rates for dollars.

Like its sister American firms, ABC Company is discouraged by the price advantage foreign companies can attain. ABC's founders would like to repeat the strategy that gave them a competitive advantage in the 1960s. Increasingly the CEO talks of another "rocket ride." Amidst hard-line discussions of ways to meet competitors head on, the CEO dreams of another invention that would create new sales opportunities and provide market dominance for another decade in a completely different product line.

This cycle, going from market dominance to market-share erosion to new market dominance, is a common American approach to maintaining competitive advantage. Unfortunately, it does not always work. A recent study by Shell Corporation, for example, found that a full third of the Fortune 500 industrials listed in 1970 had vanished by 1983 (de Geus 1988). It is difficult to sustain profitability while undergoing this cycle.

TOWARD A NEW
STRATEGY OF GLOBAL COMPETITION

Competitors in the world market, particularly the Japanese, have demonstrated a more adaptive strategy. Using the principle of *Kaizen*, or continuous improvement, the Japanese have incrementally refined American innovations, like the VCR, to the point where the Japanese now hold undisputed competitive advantage in markets where American businesses pioneered technological breakthroughs.

This continual improvement approach is not solely Japanese, however. Arie de Geus (1988) and his colleagues at Shell found that the few Fortune 500 companies that survived 75 years or longer continually ran experiments and explored new business and organizational opportunities "in the margin." These survivors were not content with harvesting profits from an unchanging product line.

Recently *Fortune* magazine concluded that *"the most successful corporation of the 1990s will be something called a learning organization"* (Domain 1989). Firms constructed as learning organizations will be able to transform experiences in doing business with their customers into new knowledge about how to do business better the next time.

Peter Senge (1990) of the Massachusetts Institute of Technology states that, as learning organizations, enterprises must now generate improvements based on customer preferences. *"You could never produce the Mazda Miata solely from market research. It required a leap of imagination to see what the customer might want"* (Senge 1990, 8). If General Electric had asked its customers in 1890 for suggestions on how to improve cold food storage, GE would probably have received descriptions of a better icebox. Few if any customers would have had the vision to describe a refrigerator. The globally competitive organization will be a learning enterprise with imaginative responses to customer needs and wants, even when the customer cannot clearly articulate them. It will sense and respond to latent needs. It will measure total quality more as a response to customer requirements and less as strict conformance to contract standards.

If American companies like ABC Company are to maintain competitive advantage in the 1990s, they must continually improve their product lines by soliciting constructive feedback from customers. Often customer "murmurs" contain insightful, creative suggestions for product improvement. For example, about 75 percent of recent innovations in scientific instruments have come from users (Dertouzos, Lester, and Solow 1990). In other words, manufacturers should not only pay attention to the needs of their customers but also learn from customer ideas, suggestions, complaints, and modifications. By establishing feedback loops with their customers, the ABC companies of America can focus on pressing business problems and reassess the self-sealing beliefs about their products that deter improvement. This learning strategy is essential to maintaining competitive advantage in the 1990s.

A NEW STRATEGY IN EDUCATION & TRAINING

Just as a change of business strategy is required to preserve profitability and save jobs, so too a strategy is required to prepare workers for starting jobs and to keep them abreast of job demands. The need of businesses for this change in strategy of education and training converged with existing trends to alter the timing of education and work.

As late as the 1950s, "getting an education" was a once-in-a-lifetime effort. In one alternative, a person went through high school and on to work, possibly obtaining some vocational-technical training, and was then updated on the job periodically under the employer's direction. In a second alternative, a person going into a professional or managerial career would go to college for four years and sometimes continue through a master's or doctorate. Thereafter, any further learning required would come about informally through professional journals, workshops, or conferences. A return to formal study in a college or university was relatively infrequent among adults.

During the 1960s, younger students began to "stop out" of school for periods of several months to several years, returning to college classrooms as nontraditional learners. Before long, legions of older adults joined this nontraditional learner group on a part-time basis. The increasing knowledge base required for career advancement provided an incentive for many adults with high-school and limited postsecondary experience to return to college to obtain degrees. But others returned to alternative institutions or found the needed new skills and knowledge within their employers' training division. Expanding employment options for women prompted many who previously had been denied the opportunity for postsecondary education to seek college degrees. Other social changes, like the increase of single-parent families, led adults to the college classroom to obtain the credentials necessary for higher-paying jobs.

The result of these changes is that 60 percent of undergraduate headcount enrollments in 1989 were adults 23 or older (NCES 1990). The proportion is continuing to increase. To meet this shift in the nature of the student population, the learning system had to change. At the same time, by 1985 five to six times as many corporate dollars were being spent on employer-provided training as on school-based instruction (Carnevale 1986).

Research on adult learners prompted further changes in the learning system. The first large-scale study of learning in adulthood disclosed that most adult learning is self-initiated (Johnstone and Rivera 1965). Confirming research showed that the average adult spent over 500 hours each year completing at least seven different major learning projects, ranging from learning how to be healthier to learning how to repair cars, build a house, or run a family business (Tough 1979). The strategy for serving adult learners expanded from a singular focus on classroom programs to multiple emphases on increased learning options for adults both in and out of the classroom.

The next influence requiring an expanded learning system is imbedded in the shifting characteristics of a skilled and productive workforce for the United States. In times past, companies could meet the need for more highly qualified workers by hiring young people just emerging from high school, college, or graduate school. Today their numbers are smaller, and they constitute a smaller proportion of the workforce than before. Of the people who will be employed in the year 2000, over 75 percent are already in the workforce (Dole 1989; U.S. Dept. of Labor 1987). Far fewer jobs today can be adequately filled by people with only an eighth-grade or even a twelfth-grade education. To meet the anticipated skill needs of the 1990s and beyond, the U.S. economy will require a massive training and retraining program for the existing workforce.

Still another influence requiring new partnerships for the learning system is the rapid creation of knowledge and information. Within the next ten years, the knowledge base underlying technology will increase by 100 percent (NCEE 1990). This change means that even those who are qualified as they come out of high school or college will not be qualified within five to ten years for the jobs opening at that time unless they have been learning during the interim.

Finally, the expanded learning system must take account of the increasing number of adults who exist on the fringes of the job market because of inadequate reading and computational skills. While many of our competitors in highly developed economies can draw on a workforce with literacy rates above 95 percent, in the United States one out of every seven adults is hampered by some degree of functional illiteracy. With the increasing technological and information processing skills required for skilled employment, the gap between the "haves" and the "have-nots" is widening too rapidly.

A GOVERNMENT FRAMEWORK FOR COMPETITIVENESS & EMPLOYABILITY

In the old perspective, America was stronger than other nations economically. It needed only modest protection from unfair competition abroad and at home and only minimal internal controls on commerce and competition. The new outlook is that competition is global and that collaboration among employers, unions, and government to yield employment security and entre-preneurial competitiveness cannot be achieved without a stable climate that rewards success as enterprises define it. Most important, the new outlook foreshadows the need to orchestrate state and federal responses to societal change. We need a national policy on human resource development.

This new view of the role of government action arises out of these basic changes in our economic and learning systems. Jerry Miller (1989), a long-time leader in efforts to expand educational opportunity and fair access to it, declares that the United States is essentially without a human resource development policy. Miller's thesis is that formal schooling, while remaining the core of human resource development, must be made to fit into a holistic national strategy for reaching and sustaining the quality needed in the ever-changing workforce. This will alter the monopolistic position of schools and colleges *"to allow other HRD providers to make their critically important contributions in an environment as free as possible of unwarranted marketplace advantages"* (1989, 1-2).

Miller also argues that an alternative credentialing system is needed, one that is based on certification of individuals, not of institutions or educational programs. How that strategy can work is discussed in Chapter 6. Initiating policies like these would, of course, require significant change of some institutions currently in place and the construction of others. This example, however, illustrates that many current practices inhibit or prohibit patterns of practice needed to optimize employability of the workforce.

In Chapter 7 we identify key governmental initiatives needed to create an infrastructure that will facilitate the new strategies of business competitiveness, employment security, and an education and learning system to match. First, however, we turn to this question: How can we identify incentives that will make the development of employability within a high performance economy an attractive prospect for all of the essential partners: industry, labor, workers, educators, and government?

2

PARTNERSHIPS FOR EMPLOYABILITY: A WIN-WIN SCENARIO

PART 2

covers the basic components needed to achieve employability.

Chapter 3

identifies the two primary systems of education and training through which workers can acquire the skills and knowledge they need to attain employability and describes how they complement each other.

Chapters 4 through 7

explain the roles of each of the major players in the employability effort: employers, workers and unions, education providers, and the federal and state governments. These chapters highlight the sometimes difficult adjustments each partner will have to make to achieve positive change. Most importantly, they emphasize the need for a sustained and coordinated effort on the part of all these partners and explain how such an effort will truly benefit them all.

TWO APPROACHES
TO EMPLOYABILITY EDUCATION

Two kinds of programs have proven their value as means to helping workers achieve the goal of employability. They are employee
growth and development programs (EGDPs) and work settings as
learning environments (WSLEs). These two arrangements, when
offered together, provide a continuum for learning by workers.
Toward one end of the continuum, EGDPs maximize learning
opportunities within the educational system. On the other end,
WSLEs provide opportunities for learning in the workplace.
Workers must have the skills to do their jobs and must work in settings that support the use of their skills (Porter and Lawler 1968).
EGDPs help workers develop the skills they need to be productive. WSLEs reinforce those skills, provide practice in applying
them, and help develop new, complementary skills. Both are
necessary for employability.

EMPLOYEE GROWTH
& DEVELOPMENT PROGRAMS

Employee growth and development programs, as noted in
Chapter 2, originated in the automotive industry in response to
the massive layoffs of 1978-82. After sometimes bitter and pro-
longed bargaining, both employers and unions realized that the

industry would not regain its earlier levels of employment soon. A solution emerged: Companies would allocate part of the money that would have been spent on wage increases, capital outlays, and benefits to an employee fund. This fund would both help laid-off workers qualify for and find work elsewhere and prepare those currently employed for a less difficult transition to new employment if downsizing occurred again.

Since 1984, CAEL has developed over thirty "joint ventures programs," or employee growth and development programs (EGDPs). CAEL designs each program individually, working with company and union partners to identify and respond to their specific needs. Until 1991 CAEL worked primarily with large employers in the industrial and service sectors, but of late has expanded its work with small businesses. Together, its programs have enabled CAEL to serve workers with widely varying levels of educational attainment and needs. The industries served range from telecommunications and paper manufacturing to candy-making, construction, and even government agencies at both the federal and state levels. In the eight years of this CAEL service, more than 30,000 workers out of an eligible EGDP population of more than 250,000 have benefited directly.

These EGDPs typically include four essential components: (1) prepaid tuition and educational fees for both active and laid-off workers; (2) employer-funded career planning and educational planning services to help workers take advantage of tuition assistance; (3) relocation assistance for laid-off workers; and (4) administrative services to provide individual assistance in workers' use of these benefits.

In time, further implications and applications of this basic idea became clear. First, the workers, not the employers, determined what education and training they would receive. An employer could still mandate training for a designated group of employees to achieve its own goal, as did Ford, for example, in 1985 in St. Louis when it geared up workers to use new technologies to produce a new kind of truck. Funds were set aside for an

EGDP in addition to the traditional in-house training programs performed on paid time. The EGDP funds were used *on the employee's own time and for the employee's choice of learning.*

In this system, the individual employee becomes personally responsible for his or her own education and training that is not mandated by the employer.

Under the old system, by guaranteeing lifelong employment and in-house training when needed for that purpose, the automakers and the unions in effect removed the responsibility for job-seeking from workers' shoulders. Having foresworn this role, employers were notifying their workers that they themselves would hereafter be responsible for getting and keeping their own jobs.

The unions were telling members that unions could not prevent this change but could obtain the financial means and the counseling support to help workers adjust to it. The union might also add that members would thereby be more independent, more in charge of their fate and fortunes than under the older, paternalistic system.

WORK SETTINGS AS LEARNING ENVIRONMENTS

A problem that has confounded educators, staff developers, and corporate trainers over the years is how to transfer learning acquired in a classroom setting to a work setting.

Workers indicate that classroom learning alone does not give them the competencies they need to do their jobs (Sternberg 1987). At best, it introduces learners to new ideas, provides them with alternate frameworks for solving problems, encourages them to expand their perspectives on the world, and increases their self-confidence in new situations. Once learners exit the classroom, they are on their own as they grapple with how to apply what they learned on the job. In many cases, only minimal transfer from the classroom to the job setting occurs.

A study by the University of Connecticut's Research Center for Organizational Learning in a large insurance company found that the impact of training on job performance was limited. In fact, several participants interviewed only three months after the training session could not even remember taking the course — let alone use the content to improve their job performance.

When workers are asked how they learned to do their jobs, they say formal classroom learning usually provides only a foundation of skills or knowledge for their current level of competence (Baldwin and Ford 1988). For individuals to develop employability, their work settings should support the use of the skills and knowledge they gain in classroom settings. This supportive combination is not easy to achieve.

The following case scenario describes a combined program developed by a firm that had provided an extensive training opportunity for employees but had realized few productivity gains. QED Engineering is a large multinational corporation that designs and manufactures a wide variety of structural systems (e.g., a trash-to-energy plant). The firm installed a three-dimensional (3-D) computer-assisted design (CAD) process as a component of a companywide computer-integrated manufacturing (CIM) system. The company invested over $100,000 in hardware and software for the 3-D CAD system. It also cycled 20 CAD operators through an eight-month training program provided by the vendor. Two years later the employer had realized only limited returns on this substantial investment of time and money. The CAD operators were having great difficulty using the capabilities of the 3-D system to address day-to-day business problems. They knew how to use the system, but because of situational constraints they could not apply it to the company's design processes. Their supervisors offered no assistance, since they knew designing as a paper-and-pencil drafting process and did not know the CAD system. Understandably, the supervisors were reluctant to attend lengthy training sessions just to figure out how to use the system more productively.

To resolve the difficulty, the CAD squads were designed as learning teams. The supervisors were trained in managing and promoting workplace learning. As each team accepted a new piece of work, the supervisors raised two questions: How can we accomplish this work most profitably? How can we learn from doing this job so that our next job will be done more productively? Slowly the CAD squads began realizing productivity gains as they worked collaboratively to develop common symbol libraries for items such as pipes or girders, skeletal frameworks that could readily be adapted to other designs, and solutions to problems caused by procedural rules that restricted applications of the 3-D CAD system. When they ran into problems beyond their collective expertise, they learned how to define their needs to make best use of the capabilities of the internal training experts and outside training consultants.

This case scenario illustrates how employees who have the knowledge and motivation to do a job can be frustrated by a work environment that does not support them in applying their skills and knowledge to current and local business problems. By turning the workplace into a learning environment, QED Engineering is slowly beginning to realize productivity gains from the 3-D CAD program.

This scenario also raises an important point regarding employee motivation to work. A popular viewpoint is that U.S. productivity has plummeted due to a decline in the American work ethic. To the contrary, a recent study by the MIT Commission on Productivity in America concluded that U.S. workers produce as well and as much as workers anywhere in the world (Dertouzos, Lester, and Solow 1989).

Even in the automobile industry, in which the Japanese are by most measures beating the Americans, American workers are able to produce as

> *much and as well as Japanese workers when the*
> *Americans are in plants set up and managed by*
> *Japanese. ... In other industries, workers in plants*
> *owned and managed by American companies are as*
> *productive as any in the world, but these are compa-*
> *nies with human resource systems that incorporate*
> *many of the best practices of Japanese and German*
> *firms* (Dertouzos, Lester, and Solow 1989, 81).

The conclusions of the MIT study, as well as the implications of the case scenario, suggest that organizations intent on gaining competitive advantage through the growth and development of their workforce cannot be content with developing skills in classroom settings alone. Corporations must encourage the growth and development of workers by enabling them to apply skills and knowledge learned in the classroom to day-to-day business problems in the workplace.

BUILDING WIN-WIN PARTNERSHIPS

The solution to achieving maximum employability seems simple: Classroom and workplace learning must reinforce each other to be fully effective. In spite of the compelling importance of employability and the central role of a new learning system in promoting universal employability, experience tells us that the weight and importance of the vision by itself will not convince all partners to participate. For the partnerships to work, all partners must gain critical advantages in the process of working together to achieve the common goal of universal employability. Chapters 4 through 7 explain how to achieve such a win-win scenario.

EMPLOYERS AS PARTNERS

WHY PARTICIPATE?

Why should an employer have an employability program? First, it yields a net reduction of personnel costs. Second, the employer gets added benefits if the program is tailored to the firm's specific situation. Third, the sum of cost reduction and added benefits nets a gain in cost effectiveness. Finally, since an employability program provides benefits to workers and the larger economy, it creates a win-win situation for everyone involved and is sustainable on an ongoing basis.

HOW TO GET THE BENEFITS?

No two employers answer this question in precisely the same way. Consider four different scenarios: 1) an aging workforce with declining productivity and competition forcing higher productivity; 2) rapid turnover of young, entry-level employees in a highly competitive field; 3) a collective bargaining situation combining downsizing for technology-based gains and concurrent starts of new subsidiary enterprises; and 4) a set of small businesses with limited means for employee development. Figures 4.1 through 4.4 summarize the costs and benefits of an employability program in these four situations.

Figure 4.1

HOW EMPLOYERS BENEFIT
FROM EMPLOYABILITY PROGRAMS

The Concept

- A win-win strategy for all stakeholders

- A net reduction of personnel costs

- Added benefits if program is tailored to employer's own situation

- Evaluating the balance of costs & benefits, a net gain

Situation 1

Declining Productivity of Aging Workforce;
Competition Forcing Higher Productivity per Worker

Major Paper Manufacturer

Benefits	Costs
Avoid:	■ Outreach expense
■ Rising disability costs	■ Counseling hours
■ Early retirement costs	■ Tuition (all levels)
■ Rising health benefits costs	■ Organizing special classes
■ Reduced productivity (from "staying on")	■ Program administration
■ Legal risks (age discrimination)	
■ Outplacement costs	

SITUATION 1:
DECLINING PRODUCTIVITY, RISING COMPETITION

Consider first a leading paper manufacturer that owns and harvests its own forests. When a timberlands worker (97 percent of these workers are males) reaches his late 30s, he is like a professional football player in the twilight of his career. His muscles have lost their resiliency. He may have some strained tendons and mended bones. He is more subject to health hazards. He bruises more easily and is more likely to need time off from work. One employer in the paper industry had records of the loss of productivity of workers over the age of 40. The cost was threatening the competitiveness of the enterprise.

If the company laid off some of these workers, it normally incurred severance expenses considerably greater than those for employees resigning voluntarily or retiring at the usual age of 62. If the terms of the severance were not amicable, there were litigation costs; the company risked losing an occasional case and incurring considerable penalties. This employer determined that an employability program would save the company money by avoiding severance and litigation costs. Additional savings in wages accrued as some employees resigned to set up their own small businesses, to enter other lines of work, or to move to more skilled jobs elsewhere in the corporation. The corporation estimated the cost of the employability program as only 30 percent of the benefits realized.

SITUATION 2:
RAPID TURNOVER, HOT COMPETITION

Consider the problem of turnover experienced by the food service industry. In some fast-food chains there is a turnover of 200 percent per year in entry-level positions. The costs of mistakes made by inexperienced workers, of constant recruiting, of initial training for the new recruits, and of accounting and administration for this volume of personnel change are substantial.

It occurred to a union leader that a frank admission to new employees that the jobs are not promising for career development, combined with an offer of education benefits that would qualify the new employee for better jobs elsewhere, could benefit employer, union, and employee. An employee who accepted the challenge to complete a certificate or degree with a community college would need to stay with the employer for one or two years, thereby doubling or quadrupling the usual length of service. The worker would gain leverage for better wages and greater employment security later in return for living with the less gratifying job for the present. The employer would save enough money on recruiting and training and on improved performance to more than offset the costs of educational benefits. Each partner would win.

Figure 4.2

Situation 2

Rapid Turnover of Entry-level Employees

Fast-food Outlets, Entry-level Jobs at Mall Retailers

Benefits	Costs
■ Lower recruiting costs for new employees	■ Counseling hours
■ Lower training costs for new employees	■ Tuition (community-college levels)
■ Reduced losses from inexperienced workers	■ Administrative cost of program management

---

SITUATION 3:
COLLECTIVE BARGAINING &
DOWNSIZING WHILE ADDING NEW SUBSIDIARIES

Employers whose compensation package is reached via collective bargaining go into bargaining with a target in mind. This target includes wages, taxes on wages, pension benefits, health-care benefits, life insurance benefits, amenities provided to employees, and other costs customary in that business as elements of compensation. Rarely does an employer get exactly what it hopes for in the total, but generally both sides are willing to trade off some benefits for others. Work rule changes, benefits likely to attract wanted employees, and other options may arise in bargaining intended to enhance overall productivity.

Figure 4.3

Situation 3

Need for Downsizing to Allow Technology-based Gains in Efficiency & Enable Starts on New Subsidiary Enterprises; Unionized, Bargaining Triennially

Major Telecommunications Companies

Benefits	Costs
■ Avoid high severance or early retirement costs	■ Outreach costs
■ Avoid new training costs in-house to upgrade workforce	■ Counseling & Returning to Learning® workshop costs
■ Other benefits would cost more if there were no educational benefits	■ Tuition (all levels)
■ Work rules can be renegotiated to gain efficiency	■ Program administration
■ Workforce becomes more productive without employer's paying for study time	

In the bargaining context, an employability program for workers can be especially attractive for an employer. Even when there is no direct link between employability training and a worker's immediate job (for example, an assembly-line worker may take an English composition course), the employer benefits from supporting the learning because it results in a more satisfied, more loyal employee who in some respects is more competent and productive. The employer also gets an employee with improved chances of advancing with the company or getting work elsewhere at a time of ongoing layoffs without the usual level of severance expense.[1] And this learning happens on the employee's own time — a savings often larger than the cost of in-house training.

In other words, employability programs are excellent investments because the money spent on education and training is an investment in human capital, an investment that will in the aggregate improve productivity (Carnevale 1982). The employee has also shared in its cost by taking less of some other benefit to include this one in the bargained package.

The automobile industry's funding of EGDPs after 1982 was the precedent for Situation 3 in telecommunications. The auto industry was dealing not only with downsizing to cope with loss of market share but also with the need for greater productivity through automation of manufacturing processes. To automate, it was necessary to introduce work teams of more highly skilled workers. A similar strategy has been used since 1989 in advanced development in computer hardware and software.

SITUATION 4:
SMALL BUSINESSES WITH TIGHT MARGINS

Large companies like those discussed in the first three scenarios not only must plan strategically to ensure their access to a qualified workforce but can afford to do so. These companies usually have staff whose job is to plot demographic trends, determine long-term training needs for a future beyond the next annual report, and plan future workforce development strategies.

This is not the case for small businesses, dynamic enterprises that fuel the economy by creating new jobs and products but that are driven by the bottom line of the present. They generally prosper by hiring the skills they need. If, for example, you are

---

1. Voluntary departures lower aggregate severance costs, and damages collectible by involuntarily laid-off workers are likely to be lower because of their enhanced prospects for other work. Severance costs include severance pay, unemployment insurance, job counseling, and hiring replacements.

Figure 4.4

Situation 4

Small Business with Minimal Funds for Employee Development

Employers with Few Employees

Benefits	Costs
■ Costs per employee are not fixed	■ Costs of specific services used
■ Can retain or upgrade proven employees	■ Broker service cost
■ Avoid more costly training	■ Any other employee education costs employer chooses to pay
■ Costs are shared by owner of corporate park or association of businesses	

---

a small business owner who needs unique software, you find a software specialist to write it. If you are a small business owner who needs to develop protocols for research on new drugs, you hire an M.D. or a Ph.D. with the appropriate experience. If you need a secretary, you look for one who knows your company's word-processing program.

Consider the limited training options available to you as a small business owner. When times are good, you send your top managers to management seminars. When money is tight, you survive with their existing skills. If your technician's understanding of electronics is inadequate to produce the product, you replace him or her with another technician. If the sales force isn't producing, you hire replacements. In-house, custom-designed training rarely occurs at all. When it does, it is usually highly specific, addressing just those skills immediately needed to transfer to a new spreadsheet system or to operate and maintain a new technology. You have allocated no funds for tuition for employees' use. Indeed, you do not even have stated tuition reimbursement policies. Each request is handled on an individual basis, and favoritism is rampant.

This haphazard nonsystem of personnel development works fine as long as there is a large, well-trained workforce available. In the late 1980s, however, when it became difficult in some parts of the country to replace a secretary or a line manager whose skills were shaky, even small companies began to realize that it might cost less in time and money to train the employees they had rather than look for new ones. But could a small business initiate an effective human resource development program to meet this training problem?

In Great Valley Corporate Center in southeast Pennsylvania, where tenants comprise a cross-section of the new service and technology economy, the answer is "Yes, but not alone." The developer of the park is consciously trying to build the workplace of the future. It has given space and start-up support to a nonprofit Business Development and Training Center (BDTC). This organization serves the needs of over 400 companies, most of which have fewer than 20 employees each.

The BDTC is housed in an old farmhouse centrally located within the complex. The BDTC acts as an education and training broker for all interested firms in the park. The BDTC's computer applications courses, other classes, and an MBA program offered at the farmhouse by a local university allow people who work in the corporate center to get the training they need during or after work hours without the additional time and expense of traveling into the city.

The BDTC offers such additional development needs for small businesses as meeting space, conference services, executive roundtables, a consultant resource file, an annual job/trade fair, personnel recruitment, placement and outplacement, and group health insurance. The BDTC can tailor its programs and services to the specifications of each employer. For example, some employers prepay tuition; some reimburse employees after courses are completed; some do not pay at all. The BDTC is flexible enough to accommodate these and more complicated differences.

When a generalized training need is identified, the BDTC may offer a generic course so that a company with limited financial resources can send one or two people. For example, many of the biotech and other high-tech companies in the corporate center were having difficulty finding employees with experience in "clean room" techniques. The BDTC found an expert instructor and worked with him to create a clean room design and maintenance course that was attended by 46 people from 22 different companies. The BDTC contracted with the same instructor to do a follow-up clean room seminar for nine employees at one of the participating companies that wanted additional product-specific training.

How do the employers benefit? Essentially, the BDTC provides a cost-effective, readily available menu of choices for the companies at the corporate center. Having a common service broker for employee development and for other business services enables each business to use the combination it considers optimal for its own purposes. The developer and the management of the corporate center also benefit, of course, because the BDTC has proved a powerful means of attracting and retaining tenants.

In other states, a comparable function of brokering and orchestrating employee growth and development services has been managed by a chamber of commerce or another form of consortium of small businesses. In Chicago, a citywide pilot venture with foundation help is under way to address small businesses' need for highly productive workers to enable them to compete in the global economy. To the best of our knowledge, however, there are few fully developed EGDP services among small businesses.

GETTING THE ADDED BENEFITS

Upon hearing these cases, a leading British business consultant said British employers would be interested only in the saving on personnel costs and not at all in "buying" other benefits at whatever bargain. Magaziner and Patimkin (1989), on the other hand, report positive effects from employee training among American employers: on profitability, loyalty to company, reduced turnover, and output per worker.

Different kinds of education save employer costs in different ways. Literacy education can reduce accidents and hazardous practices derived from nonreading. Training in interpersonal skills can reduce counterproductive office tensions, derail intra-office controversy, and improve customer relations. Advanced knowledge of the sciences is indispensable for industries where lack of expertise can result in poor product performance or dangerous products. Some kinds of education contribute to the invention of new products and services. To particular businesses, these or other direct benefits of more knowledgeable and competent employees become crucial to profitability, either on a continuing basis or at critical junctures in the development of their enterprises. Some of these benefits are provided by the training division of a corporation or through contracting for customized services. An employability program complements those means.

WHAT IF AN EMPLOYER IS COMMITTED TO CHEAP LABOR?

If a corporation seeks to become a high performance workplace, it must adopt some form of employee development program. But what if the corporation opts instead to deskill its jobs to the ultimate degree feasible, to hold down the pay levels for employees, and to turn away from any effort to become a high performance work organization? Will outlays for employee development benefit such firms?

Earlier in this chapter we recounted the experience of fastfood stores in a major metropolitan area where education benefits overcame a serious turnover problem. A somewhat different approach to providing skills training for lower-paid workers is occurring in the programs of Dusco Community Services, Inc. (DCS). In the DCS TRAC/USA© program, the employer pays a portion of the costs of prospective employee growth and development.

DCS recruits high school juniors and seniors (as well as unemployed persons in state and local training programs), including young people "at risk" whose vocational training is minimal and whose goals and expectations are undefined. They take part in a school-to-work transition program that combines completing their high-school degree with training and supervised work experience. The DCS TRAC/USA program is based in large retail malls and the work experience is largely in retailing and hospitality, but the skills base is broad and transferable to a number of other career paths.

The major difference between TRAC/USA and other work-study programs is the "intentionality" of the training. Also, a group of mentors in the worksites, senior salespersons or managers, are responsible for assuring that the work placement is a learning experience that enables the students to acquire a series of structured competencies.

What the employers get from the TRAC/USA program goes far beyond the convenience of having part-time employees whom someone else has recruited and trained. The employers are asked to think seriously about how they can change the image of retailing jobs. Traditionally these jobs have low status and low pay. They require long hours, including nights and weekends, and the career ladder is ill defined. Consequently, as the available workforce shrinks, the number of applicants for retailing jobs shrinks even further (as witness the profusion of help-wanted signs on store windows).

TRAC/USA professionalizes retailing. It helps not only the students but the mentors define their professional identity and acquire the skills base necessary to increase their productivity (and to earn more competitive wages). It concentrates on retailing not as a static job but as a career with possibilities for employees to move into roles as sales specialists, mentors of new sales associates, buyers or managers or owners. Thus, TRAC/USA makes retailing more attractive to employees and serves a long-range recruitment and retention function. The program also enhances the long-term employability of the participants.

These examples show that even low-skill worksites can benefit from employee development programs. Employers using a well-designed approach can enhance the employability of low-skilled workers, helping to increase the productivity of the American workforce.

SPECIFIC COSTS OF EMPLOYABILITY PROGRAMS

We have reviewed the ways diverse employers can benefit from employee development programs. But what must the employer contribute for an employability program to work?

Costs of an employability program to an employer-union partnership can be discussed in terms of (1) the maximum allowable sum available to an eligible person, (2) the average actual payout per eligible person, and (3) the average payout per user. In the programs with which CAEL has helped, engaging employees in formal educational programs has rarely exceeded 35 percent participation within a year. Normally participation is between 12 and 20 percent.

By 1988 the AT&T-CWA-IBEW Alliance for Employee Growth and Development had adopted an allowance of $3.75 per month per union-represented worker who was employed. By mid-1990 over 5,700 employees were in prepaid college credit tuition programs in over 325 colleges and universities and had used over $3 million for the tuitions (Ferman et al. 1991, 35, 49). UAW-Ford reported 14 percent participation in 1988 for the unduplicated headcount (15,000 in number) of the combined personal development and educational training and assistance programs (Ferman et al. 1991, 62). By contrast, two percent per year was the maximum ever achieved during the previous 20 years (1964-83) of the unilaterally administered hourly employee tuition refund program at Ford (Ferman et al. 1991). While this result is dramatic compared with the average of three to four percent per year among Fortune 500 corporations, it is not high enough to keep the American workforce current and productive.

The actual expenditure per employee varies widely in CAEL-assisted programs. By 1988 the maximum allocation per eligible employee in the UAW-Ford programs had risen to $2,550 per year. At least one CAEL-assisted program in 1991 set no specific limit per person. Since the sheer time commitment to studies limits the amount of tuition and other benefits a worker can use while fully employed, a limit of $1,500 for tuition and fees was typical.

Average costs per entitled employee have ranged from $280 per year in the early years of one program to a high of $1,001 per year. In the first instance, the cost for employees actually using the program (about 20 percent of the eligibles) was some $1,400 per year (five times the cost per eligible person).

Costs vary widely because the terms chosen by the bargaining partners vary widely to fit their particular circumstances, needs, and priorities. The basis for defining the aggregate fund available thus also varies widely. The UAW-Ford allotment was originally a nickel an hour worked by eligible employees plus 50 cents an hour for overtime. As has usually occurred with successful programs, this figure rose in subsequent bargaining. In many partnerships, the basic tuition assistance program is supplemented by other offerings (assistance to laid-off workers, retirement planning services, special-purpose workshops, spouse benefits, leadership education, and more). Finally, considerable costs of developing, administering, monitoring, and evaluating the programs and of outreach and promotional efforts must be added to reflect total costs accurately.

Costs are affected by the list of benefits and services included within the employee development program. Employers and their partners typically choose only some of the many benefits possible, but a few jointly administered programs have used the entire set listed below and have, as might be expected, enjoyed the highest participation rates. In the comprehensive programs, advocacy and administrative services for a large workforce may be as low as 20 to 25 percent of costs, while the lion's share of costs are in prepaid tuition benefits. A typical CAEL EGDP menu includes:

■ Outreach services

■ Prepaid tuition

■ Pre-enrollment advising, career planning, and education planning

■ Follow-up advising and counseling

■ Returning to Learning® workshops

■ Regular fees other than tuition

■ Books

■ Administrative services

The ultimate test of the costs of EGDPs is whether they reduce other costs or add a range of benefits that represents a bargain for the buyer. CAEL clients have typically renewed their contracts for the EGDP service because these two tests show that the service enhances their net profits.

TRAINING AS AN OVERALL BUSINESS STRATEGY

According to the MIT Commission on Productivity in America (Dertouzos, Lester, and Solow 1989), the decline of American productivity is due more to the organizational and attitudinal deficiencies of numerous American businesses (e.g., use of outdated strategies, adherence to short time horizons, failure to cooperate with suppliers and customers) than to such macroeconomic influences as exchange rates, interest rates, tax laws, and import quotas.

Among the counterproductive attitudes the MIT Commission found in American businesses were the continued neglect of human resources and the failure to cultivate employee skills to increase productivity. American businesses repeatedly claim, "We have no training problem in our company."

> *In Italy we observed highly trained loom operators working together with fabric designers to exploit the technical possibilities of the loom and to dream up new products. In the United States we heard a prominent textile manufacturer boast that only the top manager in the plant knew how to set up the looms and that the operators; "guys down from the hills who are good at fixing cars," did not need any special training to work on them* (Dertouzos, Lester, and Solow 1989, 82).

This attitude toward the skill and training needs of workers is a holdover from the days when firms set up in accord with principles of mass production treated workers as replaceable parts. The option of developing multiskilled workers was seldom pursued. Management treated workers as costs to be controlled rather than assets to be developed.

> *There seems to be a systematic undervaluation in this country of how much difference it can make when people are well educated and when their skills are continuously developed and challenged. This underestimation of human resources becomes a self-fulfilling prophecy, for it translates into a pattern of training for work that turns out badly educated workers with skills that are narrow and hence vulnerable to rapid obsolescence* (Dertouzos, Lester, and Solow 1989, 82).

Employers can realize gains from investment in training as an overall business strategy, as the following case illustrates.

LIVE CASE STUDIES

The power products division of QED Engineering was in serious trouble because of poor project management. To remedy the situation, a blue-ribbon task force decided to imbed project manager training within project review meetings. The idea was to train project managers on how to increase profit margins, improve customer relations, ensure quality, and reduce risk liability while the project managers were presenting project reviews. (One participant referred to these meetings as live case studies.) The plan took more than 24 months to implement and required many steps, including training supervisors on how to conduct project reviews as learning sessions, but the results were well worth it. During the first six months of 1990, the profit margin on projects within the division improved by four percent. During the third quarter of 1990, profit margins improved by another three percent.

In this example, management committed to training as an overall business strategy. Learning how to be a project manager shifted from a one-time event to an ongoing process. Concepts required for effective project management were introduced, clarified, and reinforced by supervisors during project review sessions. These concepts were then used to devise project management strategies. In combination, these two steps maximized the learning potential of ongoing business activities and moved the business unit closer to being a learning organization.

LEARNING ORGANIZATIONS & TOTAL QUALITY MANAGEMENT

The watchwords of today's manufacturing enterprises are "total quality management" and "time-based management." In the service sector, the correlate is "total quality service." The common theme of business strategies is continuous improvement of processes, products, and services. One manufacturing vice president described the importance of continuous improvement to his company's business strategy:

Right now we're competing with two other multi-national firms for dominance in the Japanese market. All three of our companies have quality products. All provide great service. Today we have a corner on the market because we sell the process we use to make the product along with the product itself. In the 1960s this practice would have been branded suicidal. Today it is a necessity. We are commited to continuous improvement. We believe that our own workforce will make the next genera-tion of our product so superior that our Japanese customers will buy from us again. To succeed we have to improve our product faster than the Japanese can. So far we've been successful.

With increasing pressure to improve continually, business enter-prises need to cultivate a capable workforce. Continuous improvement does not reside in new process technologies, robot-ics, or speedier computers. As one manager noted, "The music is not in the piano." Improvements in production and service occur when workers have the skills to do their jobs better and when they work in settings that support the full use of their skills and knowl-edge. Employers devoted to total quality enterprises can gain the full advantages of continuous improvement strategies only by developing a learning organization. Employee growth and devel-opment programs and worksites as learning environments that maximize the learning potential of the workplace are key to estab-lishing competitive learning organizations.

When total quality organizations conduct cost analyses, they ask, "What is the cost of noncompliance?" In a manufactur-ing business, noncompliance is assessed in terms of waste, scrap, and returned orders. In a service organization, the cost is determined by disgruntled customers who take their business elsewhere.

Employers who are weighing the advantages of establishing learning organizations and promoting the employability of the workforce can ask themselves the same type of question: What is the cost of noncompliance with continuous improvement procedures? What is the cost of squelching innovative ideas by using a constrictive hierarchy? What is the cost of the time during which the full production capabilities of new technologies are underutilized by workers? What is the cost of training that never transfers to work settings or is never used to solve business problems? What is the cost of workers who are not achieving their full productive capacity as contributing members of high-performance work teams? The answers highlight the benefits employers derive from promoting employability of the workforce.

5

WORKERS & UNIONS AS PARTNERS

Workers and their unions are essential partners for establishing and maintaining employable workers. They must address two questions to find a win-win scenario in the employability process: (1) How can workers improve their earnings and their employability by taking part in employability programs? and (2) How can a union best serve its membership and strengthen itself by committing to the lifelong employability of its members?

HOW THE WORKER BENEFITS

As mentioned in Chapter 1, employability means that an individual is qualified for currently available work, work that makes reasonably good use of the person's capabilities and provides a living wage. Employability does *not* guarantee a lifetime job with a single employer. It *does* guarantee relatively stable employment if the person also knows how to go about finding a job and is diligent and competent in doing so. For the individual worker, employability means control over his or her own destiny. It means that workers can chart their own careers without depending on the benevolence of a single employer. The defining benefit for workers in an employability program is reasonable assurance of staying employed. Figure 5.1 details the costs and benefits to workers of an employability program.

Figure 5.1

HOW WORKERS BENEFIT FROM EMPLOYABILITY PROGRAMS

What Is the Idea?

■ An investment in lifelong ability to get & hold jobs

■ A way to increase earning power

■ A route toward a more fulfilling type of work

■ A way to pay for education not otherwise affordable

■ A means of receiving academic credit for what was learned on the job

What Is the Trade-Off for Workers?

Benefits	Costs
■ Employment security	■ Time for study taken from family, recreation, etc.
■ Improved compensation over time	
■ More fulfilling work	■ Risk of failure in school
■ Prepaid tuition provided by employer	■ Potential damage to family life
■ Career planning services	■ Hard job of juggling responsibilities
■ Support services by joint venture staff	■ Trade-off of other fringe benefits or of some part of wage increase or of less stringent work rules
■ Growth in intellectual complexity & maturity	
■ Rise in self-esteem	
■ Role model for children	

In today's market, employability is most reliably achieved by a combination of formal and informal learning pursued within an individually structured learning plan that takes into account the learner's own skills, preferences, and values as well as the realities of current and emerging workforce needs. There is a range of options that employees can use to establish and promote their own employability — from being in an employee growth and development program to learning on the job to self-managed learning outside of work and school. The first two approaches give most promise.

THE EMPLOYEE GROWTH & DEVELOPMENT PROGRAM

An employee growth and development program may be supported by employers and their unions or by one or the other on its own.

The well-designed EGDP has the following components:

1. Outreach services to interest workers in the program and assist them in choosing whether and when to participate;

2. Prepaid tuition and fees, reimbursement of cost of books and materials;

3. Access to assistance in career and education planning based on knowledge of the job market and the learners' understanding of their own values, interests, and skills;

4. Access to workshops or counseling to help learners choose appropriate schools, programs, and courses and to manage the multiple constraints and responsibilities involved in coping simultaneously with the roles of student, worker, spouse, parent, and participant in community life;

5. Provision, when necessary (as in apprenticeships or in commonly needed areas such as literacy), of conveniently available classroom training (perhaps at worksite or in union hall); and

6. Advocacy services in dealing with education providers to see that employees get a good deal for the dollar expended and to help troubleshoot problems.

The options provided by an EGDP, including college courses or vendor-provided workshops, enhance a worker's employability. They help individuals develop the skills required for employability. Courses, workshops, and degree programs introduce workers to new theories and ideas, broaden the perspectives they can use in solving work-related problems, offer additional options for attaining work-unit goals, improve skills, and enhance self-confidence. (See Chapter 11 for further details about EGDPs.) Overall, participating in an EGDP can support acquisition of specific skills and competencies that enhance workers' employability and can promote their self-esteem. Worker-learners who have participated in EGDPs have described the benefits as follows:

> *With the demands of society today, it is not enough to just work in a job and get a paycheck. I want to be competitive, and when I get my education, I will be able to do that.*

> *My test-taking and thinking skills improved in the PM-ED program, and when I took a test for a promotion I passed. The Returning to Learning® workshop helped give me direction, and now my life is in high gear.*

> *Learning was always a challenge for me. Even in high school, I often squeezed by with just an average grade. But now my whole outlook on school has changed. I really want to learn and improve my life. Even my self-worth has changed. I used to think that I wasn't good enough because I only had a high school diploma. I can't express the pride and joy I felt when I received an A for the [college] English course.*

What a sense of accomplishment to know I could get such a grade!

I knew my time on the assembly line was running out. Most of my buddies had already lost their jobs, and the rumor mill said the plant would close. So with the help of CUOP [College and University Options Program], I went back to school and learned computer-aided design. I have a new job in Ford now, and I feel that my family is more secure.

Implicit in these comments is the understanding that the EGDP helps learner-workers in the following ways:

1. To get a more realistic picture of their own potential for more responsible and more remunerative work and for more advanced learning;

2. To consider a broader range of options for their future work life and to develop a heightened sense of self-esteem and self-confidence in facing and coping with the difficulties of that work life;

3. To gain access to appropriate classroom complementation for apprenticeships and literacy programs, to gain backup knowledge for workplace adoption of new technologies, and to develop needed skills to retain the current job or prepare for new jobs;

4. To improve chances of a successful career transition or advancement within a currently satisfying line of work; and

5. To support growth in the complexity and sophistication of their personal development.

These benefits also apply to people who are unemployed or who are just entering the job market.

COSTS & RISKS TO THE WORKER

It would be too good to be true if something so full of benefits had no down side. Indeed, the costs and the risks are genuine and substantial.

First, if an employer is offering an employability program, the worker has usually given up some other benefits he or she might have received. Normally, improved health benefits, further wage increases, larger child care benefits, or better pension provisions are sacrificed, at least in part.

The second most significant cost of an employability program to a worker is usually time. Employees generally use the EGDP benefits *on their own time.* Everyone has just 24 hours per day and is already using it all before the EGDP comes along. So sleep, family time, recreational time, or time for volunteering in the community is often cut down for a while. The resultant tensions mean that most full-time workers involved in an EGDP "stop in and stop out." That is, they commit to a course or two for six months, then take a term off, then return for a year, then take another term off, and so on.

Learners who choose a learning option not fully funded by the EGDP may have to make direct cash outlays. Some programs rule out personal development workshops or courses altogether; others permit partial funding. Some training programs require equipment for which the EGDP will not pay. Worst of all, federal laws and regulations sometimes tax educational benefits as ordinary employee income.

The side effects and further consequences of these sacrifices of other fringe benefits, time, and cash can add to the down side of an employability program. Occasionally a marriage breaks up, not necessarily because there is less time for the spousal relationship, but because the new autonomy of a woman who has discovered her potential for career and income through further education is a threat to her husband. (Sometimes, though, the side effects are positive, as when a husband discovers fulfillment in taking a greater share of parenting responsibilities or when a change of work rules requires teamwork from employees who used to work in a more solitary way.) But most participants in EGDPs have experienced some stresses and strains from participation in the employability program.

AN IMPORTANT ROLE FOR COLLEGE STUDIES

We warned earlier that not every college course helps a worker become more employable. While an occasional course or formal workshop under college auspices may yield immediate skill gains on a particular job, such gains may be best provided in either customized training provided by the employer or informal learning on the job. The greatest contribution of formal postsecondary studies to enhancing employability is foundational and long-term.

College studies can contribute to worker employability in three major ways. First, by helping workers learn how to learn, college studies allow them to master the tools and strategies of inquiry. Ideally, this mastery will not only lead workers to enjoy learning but encourage them to continue learning on their own as new opportunities arise. Second, a college course gives workers a foundation of knowledge of key concepts and methods in a broad field, making it easier for them to keep up with accumulating knowledge in that field. And third, a college course can enable workers to develop generic competences and capabilities related to their long-term career and personal development. This generates self-confidence and self-respect, empathy, influence skills, leadership skills, maturity in interpersonal relationships, and competence in teamwork.

LEARNING IN WORK SETTINGS

Short-term efforts to provide workers with employability skills via formal studies are most successful when complemented by a work setting that supports the development and use of those skills.

Workers play a central role in establishing, maintaining, and advancing the pace at which an organization learns. As individual workers engage actively in the learning opportunities the workplace provides, they improve their own employability and contribute to the productivity of the entire organization.

The story of Joan, outlined in the opening chapter, illustrates these benefits. Let's take a closer look at Joan's situation. She wanted to increase her skills to make sure that rapid advances in technology did not leave her with outdated qualifications. Because of her current commitments to care for her children and her earlier decision to drop out of high school in her junior year, Joan could not enroll in a degree program at the community college. Joan's supervisor on the cellular manufacturing team recognized her potential and encouraged her to learn as many skills as she could within the unit. During the two years before the layoffs, Joan rotated among a dozen different jobs within her unit.

By taking advantage of these workplace learning opportunities, Joan developed a wide range of skills in set-up procedures, assembly processes, and inventory controls that improved her employability. Because of her broad understanding of many procedures within the unit, Joan became a resident expert in reducing cycle time caused by cumbersome set-up procedures, in using process controls to improve assembly routines continuously, and in designing just-in-time inventory controls. When the layoffs occurred, Joan was hired by another company because of her expertise in these areas.

The process of gaining these skills on the worksite had many advantages for Joan. First, she learned at her own pace, using the hands-on methods she preferred. Second, her efforts had immediate benefits as she solved problems that caused her daily frustration. Third, by increasing her contributions to her team, she received gratifying reinforcement from co-workers. Her successes as a contributing team member also became sources of pride and self-esteem she had never experienced in classroom settings. Overall, Joan's worksite provided her with recognition for what she was learning and encouraged her to continue her development and to enhance her employability in the process.

There were also drawbacks to Joan's efforts that sometimes left her wishing she had never left the comfort and security of her old circumscribed job. Each time she set about learning how to perform another function within her cellular team, she had to confront her fears of failure. What made her think a high-school dropout could learn about numerical process-control procedures? Hadn't she always failed at this in school? The hardest part of the learning process for Joan was taking responsibility for herself and determining what to learn next. Unlike a classroom setting where the teacher sets the schedule, this workplace setting put Joan relatively on her own. She could count on her supervisor and co-workers for ideas and suggestions, but in the end the decisions — and the consequences — were hers.

Joan could easily have arrived at work each day, completed her job, and gone home. She did not take this easy route. Instead, she took advantage of opportunities available to her and developed an advanced set of integrated skills that ensured her future employability.

Many other workers who do not have Joan's drive and determination can also achieve the same improvement in employability within their worksetting if that setting (including supervisors, co-workers, and job tasks) is designed to support development of work skills. Joan's solo effort can become commonplace if workers are encouraged to use the workplace for continual learning.

WHAT EMPLOYABILITY MEANS TO UNIONS

When it comes to investing in the future, workers and their unions seem to face a more personal and harder set of choices than do their employers. For the individual worker, the choice is enhanced employability versus more tangible benefits like higher immediate wage increases, better health benefits, less onerous work rules, and shorter hours. This is a tough choice. To compound the difficulty for union leaders, not all members will be ready to use the benefit immediately or fully. Some may stand to benefit more than others. How can equity among members be achieved under these conditions?

Union leaders have supported employability programs for several reasons. First, they were realistic in recognizing that job security simply can no longer be sustained. Second, they have seen the need for a company to avoid losing more market share or even facing bankruptcy.

Finally, some of the best-informed union leaders have recognized that ultimately jobs can best be retained if a high performance work strategy is pursued, not one that deskills jobs. This recognition demands that a way be found to help workers upgrade their own qualifications while continuing on the job. A union that supports the skill development of its members can become known as one that represents a high-quality workforce. Indeed, there was a time in American labor history when the union label was a guarantee of product quality. This reputation can be resurrected by unions that pursue an employability strategy.

THE UNION AS ADVOCATE & GUARANTOR OF EMPLOYABILITY

If unions become advocates of universal employability and seek to enhance their members' lifelong employability, their roles will change on four fronts, according to Larry Fox, former deputy commissioner of labor in Connecticut and a lifelong union organizer.

First, unions would gain direct control of their membership. Under the present system, employers determine union membership. Once an employer hires a worker, that individual becomes eligible for union membership. The membership continues until the employer terminates employment. If unions were to attract members on the basis of lifelong employability, individuals would remain union members as they moved among jobs and companies.

Second, unions would expand their influence within the educational system. If unions became advocates of lifelong employability for their members, they could negotiate for educational services that best met members' needs. In fact, the United Auto Workers played a key role in persuading the UAW-Ford National Development and Training Center to press for on-site courses, credit for prior learning, courses offered at convenient times, customized instruction, specialized workshops, reductions in course fees, and financial aid in their College and University Options Program. This precedent has been followed by the Communications Workers of America, the International Brotherhood of Electrical Workers, and others.

Third, unions could exercise more control over the credentialing process. Currently, educational institutions have a near-monopoly on credentials. If unions became advocates of lifelong employability, they could cooperate with industry to create career paths in a craft by awarding credentials for graduated increments of expertise that represent the skill and learning outcomes of combined experience and coursework. These union- and company-sponsored credentials could provide the basis for advancement, promotion, and expanded opportunities within an occupation. The danger that such competing credentials would weaken college diplomas might induce colleges to modify their credentials and the routes to their achievement to better respond to workers' needs.

Finally, Fox argues that advocating employability would return unions to their original purpose. When John Stuart Mill first championed the union movement in the mid-1800s, he saw it as the best way to provide social justice for British workers. In an age when education, specialized skills, the ability to analyze information, the capacity to manipulate information, and the capacity to communicate in various media are required of so many workers, a union that expands its influence within the educational system and advocates the lifelong employability of its members becomes a champion of modern-day social justice.

On balance, the workforces that have had access to employability programs of the type analyzed here have strongly supported their continuance and enhancement. When union leaders and employees in the EGDPs have been surveyed, large majorities invariably voted to continue the programs. Even workers not yet participating themselves were in favor of EGDPs.

EDUCATION PROVIDERS AS PARTNERS

Despite the vast education network of company training programs, private and public training agencies, and consultants, the
established school systems — high schools, colleges, universities,
and vocational-technical schools — are still crucial to the success
of employability programs. The significance of the secondary and
postsecondary systems goes beyond the obvious fact that they are
currently society's primary educational service providers. To the
extent that they are publicly subsidized, they bear the obligation to
respond to society's emerging needs. To the extent that they define
themselves as being responsive to society's challenges, they have
the privilege of serving as agents of social change in a time of
rapidly escalating demands on all forms of education.

Employability of the workforce and competitive advantage for U.S. business can be maintained only through a *learning
system* that consists of viable partnerships among employers,
unions, workers, educational institutions, and government
agencies. Participation in this learning system presents our educational institutions with distinctive problems and opportunities. It
also challenges them to work within a framework of fair competition to support employee growth and development programs and
at the same time help businesses establish themselves as learning
organizations. Figure 6.1 summarizes how education providers
help and benefit in employability programs.

Figure 6.1

HOW EDUCATION PROVIDERS BENEFIT FROM EMPLOYABILITY PROGRAMS

What Is the Idea?

■ Optimal matching of learners to education providers yields greater learning by the students

■ Optimal matching of learners & providers is efficient for the society, advantageous to taxpayers & users

■ Partnerships in employability programs can triple to quadruple enrollments of mature adults in school & college

■ Employability programs enable education providers to fulfill a mandate for public service

HOW THE PROVIDERS HELP & BENEFIT

How They Help

■ Name liaisons to help plan & implement the cooperation

■ Make counselors available to be trained & to counsel workers

■ Provide instruction in ways maximally responsive to the needs of worker-learners

■ Temper competition by bonafide efforts to support the goal of optimal matching of learners & providers

How They Benefit

■ Increased enrollments of students who bring life & work experiences to campus classroom discussions

■ Funding for students who otherwise need financial aid

■ Financial rewards from cooperative programs with business, industry, government & labor

■ Opportunity to serve taxpayers better & enhance ties to the community

■ Opportunities for faculty & staff development

■ Opportunities for research partnerships & exchange of technology, faculty, & equipment with new partners

■ Impetus to update curricula & add new offerings

Historically, educational institutions have operated independently and have seldom entered into partnerships. But today they must think of themselves as partners in a learning system simply because of the increasing numbers of education providers.

Over the past 20 years, business and industry, government agencies, and labor unions have developed an extensive and varied array of in-house training courses and programs. Larger companies may have an elaborate (and expensive) structure of HRD managers, trainers, and, in some cases, training centers with sophisticated educational hardware and software. There are even 18 "corporate colleges" that, though created by corporate funding, have their own separate identities, award degrees, and are accredited by the same regional agencies that accredit other postsecondary institutions.

Carnevale (1986) has estimated the outlay by corporations for formal training of employees at $30 billion per year (only a bit more than a third of which is spent out of house, with colleges, universities, or others).[1] Carnevale estimates businesses' informal employee training costs at $150 billion to $180 billion per year, as compared with a total annual outlay of $238 billion for the whole of elementary, secondary, and postsecondary education. Estimates of the cost of the extra training needed in the 1990s to build a qualified workforce range from $210 to $225 billion a year, a figure some still find too low (Fowler 1990).

ARE ALL THESE PROVIDERS ESSENTIAL?

As shown in Figure 6.2, the existing learning system includes numerous providers of education and training at multiple levels. In addition to programs offered by colleges, universities, and vocational-technical schools, adults seeking to enhance their employability can find viable options within adult GED and other

---

1. Dole (1989) places this figure in perspective by noting that it represents only 1.3 percent of total payroll costs of American businesses

Figure 6.2

MATRIX OF PROVIDERS

Postsecondary

Four-Year Colleges & Universities
Degree-granting institutions offer traditional courses of study for undergraduates & graduates.

Two-Year Colleges & Degree-Granting Vocational Technical Institutes
Nearly 5 million students (including about 55% of all college freshmen) enrolled in more than 1,200 community colleges during the 1987-88 school year. Average student age is 29.

Non-Collegiate Vocational Schools
Proprietary schools, technical institutions, & specialized schools offer training in such fields as cosmetology, computers, auto & aircraft mechanics, & truck driving.

Adult Secondary

High School Carnegie Unit
Adults attend day or evening classes to earn credits. Offered in 42 states.

General Educational Development (GED)
High-school equivalency program of five tests administered by the American Council on Education. Awards one-sixth of all U.S. high-school diplomas (471,500 in 1988). Offered in 50 states.

External High School Diploma Program
Competency-based high-school diploma program credentials generalized life-skill competencies. Offered in 11 states.

Home Study
Accredited correspondence courses help adults earn high-school credit. Program offered for high-school diplomas in 13 states.

On-The-Job Instruction

Private Business & Industry Training
Formal & informal training, usually focused on occupational skills, is provided on-site & off.

Apprenticeship
Classroom instruction & hands-on learning or structured on-the-job training. Offered in over 88 trades throughout the country.

Military Training
The armed forces provide a wide range of instruction, from basic recruit training to specialized skill training.

Facilitating Programs

Federal Second-Chance Programs
Federal second-chance training programs, such as the Job Training Partnership Act (JPTA) of 1982, the Economic Dislocation & Worker Adjustment Act (EDWAA), the Job Opportunities & Basic Skills Training (JOBS) program, & the Targeted Jobs Tax Credit.

State Programs
State programs support employer-specific skill training, such as the Bay State Skills Corporation, the California Employment & Training Panel, & the Prairie State 200 Authority (Illinois).

Labor-Management Agreements
Labor-management agreements, ranging from apprenticeships to programs that train & retrain active workers [e.g., UAW-Ford, and AT&T, CWA and US WEST.]

Source: Johnston, 1989

high-school programs, on-the-job instruction, apprenticeships, the military services, and various state, federal, and union-facilitated programs (NCES 1992). Many community organizations offer adult education options in arts and crafts, the humanities, current affairs, and technical, professional and recreational areas. Are so many kinds of providers essential?

We believe they are both essential and beneficial. The country's need for education and training to meet the goal of universal employability will be achieved more easily and less expensively if each of these providers performs its distinctively best service, as demonstrated in the following cases.

Bill W. is part of a crew that goes into the woods daily to harvest trees for paper production. He is the one who repairs saws or other equipment when they fail. But Bill has only a ninth-grade education. He is now 49 years old, is losing more and more work days to on-the-job injuries, and is less able to keep pace than before. He wants to leave his present work and set up his own machine repair shop. But to do so he will need to earn a GED certificate (equivalent to a high school diploma) and to get some education on both machine repair and business management. For the GED he needs a local adult education service that is state funded and charges no tuition. Then he can learn machine repair at a vocational-technical school and take the management course at a nearby community college.

Kathy L. has already finished two years of college and has good secretarial skills, including competence in word processing. She is divorced; to support her two children, she needs better-paying work. She is employed by a large firm. Her plan is to get into management there or in another large company and work her way up. While the company provides in-house training for upgrading in her present work, the preparation for larger responsibilities will have to be done on her own time with outside providers such as one of the local private or public colleges.

Every worker needs to become and stay well enough qualified to get and hold jobs as job requirements continue to change.

The qualifications needed are a combination of academic skills, work skills, generic capabilities, and knowledge. The ideal combination of these ingredients differs from job to job. Over the course of an individual's working life, as job markets change and the worker's needs and goals change, different training needs emerge. No one kind of education provider can provide all of the needed programs and services. It is more efficient for providers to specialize and for learners to pick and choose to fit their particular needs and tastes.

A highly diverse array of education and training providers is thus essential to the employability of the workforce.

THE ROLE OF THE PUBLIC SCHOOLS

Public school bashing has become a national sport, with the schools taking the brunt of criticism of our workforce preparation system. It must be acknowledged, however, that the schools are besieged with new responsibilities arising out of changes in the nature of our society, a funding structure that favors affluent school districts over their poorer, usually urban, neighbors, and a plethora of internal and external questions about their mission, purposes, and methods. The shape and content of teaching and learning to prepare for citizenship in a rapidly changing world are in question as never before.

That having been said, we must also acknowledge that our schools are not doing as good a job as we might wish. U.S. high-school graduates consistently score lower than those of other industrialized nations in measures of verbal and numerical ability, and, as any entry-level employer will testify, they are woefully unprepared for the world of work (Brock and Marshall 1990). In an education system oriented mainly to the needs of the college bound, those high-school students not slated to go on to college are typically tracked into a watered-down general education curriculum that *"ends up providing neither strong academic skills nor strong vocational skills"* (Magaziner 1989, 44). Indeed, those who enter the workforce directly out of high school account for only 25 percent of all secondary school vocational credits (44). Many of them not only lack vocational preparation but do not understand such simple imperatives of the workplace as showing up on time and completing assigned tasks.

The use of existing educational resources to develop employability is a particularly controversial issue in the case of basic skills training. Understandably, businesses faced with high school educated workers who cannot read, write, communicate, make basic calculations, or deal with customers are skeptical about using educational institutions. "Why," they ask, "should we return to the secondary schools with a problem they have already failed to solve?" Although this logic is difficult to refute, there are promising initiatives on the horizon that argue for a second chance.

Adopt-a-school programs on the part of individuals and industries are a step in the right direction, but they are mere grains of sand on the huge beach of public education. More encouraging is recent legislation proposed in the Congress by a bipartisan group, Edward Kennedy (D-MA), Richard Gephardt (D-MO), Mark Hatfield (R-OR) and Ralph Regula (R-OH). Based on the recommendations of the Commission on the Skills of the American Workforce, the legislation calls for national performance standards for students planning to go directly from high school into the workforce; school-to-work transition programs; "second chance" programs for dropouts; and provision of a specified minimum amount of training by employers of 20 or more workers.

The U.S. Army's basic skills program arose out of the need to prepare recruits, some of them with weak high-school backgrounds, for service in a high skills, high tech fighting force. It is now widely acknowledged to be one of the most effective training programs in the country. Some if its techniques and materials might well be adapted by the public schools.

Employers today prefer entry-level workers with broad generic skills over those with only specific technical or professional skills. This preference has obvious implications for the role of vocational education in this country. The move toward defining skills and competencies more broadly is echoed in Europe, where vocational education has been in flux for some time.

In Germany, for instance, training protocols for skilled occupations have been redesigned to address a wider range of qualifications, and skills formation and personal development have been integrated holistically (Laur-Ernst 1990). The German system is based on the idea that *"the people, their wishes, goals, experiences and competencies must not be ignored. Vocational training should also contribute to personal development. ... Vocational standards should not be formulated without reflection on cultural and social changes"* (4). This same report called for an end to separation of general and vocational education and recognition of their necessary convergence. *"This degree of overlap between the general and the vocational can be expected to increase as the nature of work and work organization changes and becomes more complex"* (8).

This perspective would be regarded as fairly radical by tradition-minded vocational schools in the United States, many of which see their job as more technical than developmental. There are signs that even this segment of the learning system, however, is beginning to rethink the purpose and content of its curricula.

A NEW ROLE FOR COLLEGES & UNIVERSITIES

Colleges and universities can be valuable partners in a learning system dedicated to employability. Ideally, they can contribute three vital elements to the partnership network: expertise, learning resources, and knowledge of the learning process.

The most obvious contribution the academy can make is to make the knowledge, insight, and experience of the professoriate readily available through courses, seminars, workshops, and publications. While these packages are the most basic resource offered by colleges, in the long run the courses may be the least valuable contribution of postsecondary educational institutions to the evolving learning system. Frequently, the parceling out of knowledge into courses fits neither the needs of the workforce nor the pressing interests of business and industry.

The second, and sometimes more useful, offering of postsecondary education is learning resources, including libraries, computer centers, buildings, classrooms, and audiovisual and electronic teaching tools. At a less obvious level the resources include faculty, staff, and students who have the time, interest, and capabilities to help other partners in the learning system with employability issues.

The third, and potentially most valuable, resource offered by educational institutions is knowledge of the learning and education processes as well as how people grow and develop. Academic and career counseling assistance must be made available for workers attempting to access a complicated learning system. In the emerging technological age, when both knowledge and information are available to all members of society, the ability to acquire and use information is increasingly critical. Here the expertise of academic institutions can be put to new uses.

Unfortunately, educators seldom promote their understanding of the educative process as a valuable commodity. Likewise, the business community frequently does not see postsecondary education as an available resource to address business problems.

BARRIERS TO COOPERATION

Numerous factors work against easy collaboration between colleges and industry. The arguments against the postsecondary community are complex and frequently based on unarticulated issues of resentment of what is perceived as academic arrogance or an ivory-tower approach unsuited to workforce development. Figure 6.3 summarizes the reasons companies commonly give for not taking their training needs to the postsecondary education community. Let us consider these reasons one by one.

Figure 6.3

WHY CORPORATIONS DON'T TURN TO COLLEGES FOR THEIR TRAINING NEEDS

- Slow response time
- Lack of flexibility
- Content & method inappropriate to adult learners
- Lack of up-to-date practical & technical information
- Difficulty in getting decisions made & approved in the academic bureaucracy
- Resistance to change
- Unfamiliarity with adult students
- Restricted range of services

SLOW RESPONSE TIME

Schools' responses to requests for training are certainly slower than companies would like. While corporate managers may complain that schools cannot satisfy their request until next semester, the schools may reasonably respond that being left out of the critical early planning stages seriously impedes their ability to have their resources at the ready. Moreover, complex external demands for faculty time, scheduling changes, and new curricula put a strain on scarce academic resources that may take time to resolve.

INFLEXIBILITY

A lack of flexibility in setting hours and places for instruction is another issue that can be mitigated by both parties' involvement in early planning. The school may be asked to forgo its own semester system to deal with the varying schedules of shift workers, to do on-site academic and career counseling *before* the workers actually register for classes, and to forgo payment at registration and accept vouchers instead. It may have to rethink both the content and structure of some of its academic programs, to design new methods of delivery to reach people who could not otherwise participate, to institute a prior learning assessment program and, finally, to deal with faculty for whom teaching new students in new ways at new times and places is a less than inviting prospect. All of these complex external demands strain existing academic structures and may be resisted by unimaginative administrators.

INAPPROPRIATE TEACHING METHODS

Inadequate or inappropriate teaching methods based on faculty's lack of experience with adult learners and inattention to adult learning theory are endemic in some institutions. By the mid-1980s, however, most postsecondary institutions welcomed the increasing numbers of adults on campus. As adults have become the norm rather than the exception, faculty have become more concerned about developing new teaching strategies and methods of delivery to adapt to diverse learning needs and styles.

INAPPROPRIATE CONTENT

As for the complaint about professors' lack of up-to-date technical information or lack of practical experience in their fields, there is probably a mixture of truth and fiction here. Faculty careers and reputations in science and in technical and professional fields are built on their keeping abreast of the newest theories and information in their fields, and, in fact, contributing to the state of knowledge through research and writing. While not all faculty continue to seek opportunities for practical experience, many professors earn handsome stipends by consulting for some of the very executives who scoff at the academic ivory tower mentality. Closer partnerships between schools and industry would give all those who teach a broader window on the working world.

LACK OF TIMELY DECISIONS

The complaint about the difficulty of getting decisions made in the academic bureaucracy is often justified. Most postsecondary institutions' experience dealing with business and industry is most frequently limited to fairly simple transactions in which the school "sells" a course to a business. Negotiations for such transactions usually focus on issues of price and time of delivery.

The demands on the institution from an employability program with a major employer may be much more complicated and raise new issues of financial responsibility, appropriate use of resources, and program control. Businesspeople's complaints about difficulties getting decisions made and approved are frequently justified. Again, the solution lies in establishing long-term partnerships, not just for the purpose of delivering a single course or program but for recreating the nature of the educational transaction between businesses and the colleges.

RESISTANCE TO CHANGE

The perception that postsecondary institutions have an ingrained resistance to change must in some instances be taken quite seriously. Although American faculty tend to be politically liberal, they can become very conservative if they fear that the nature and functions of higher education are in danger of change through an outside agent. Their concerns about the sanctity of traditional academic content and the dangers of pragmatism must be thoughtfully addressed if resistance to change is to be overcome.

UNFAMILIARITY WITH ADULT STUDENTS

Adult worker-learners in employability programs may prove a challenge to many faculty members. Until recently, most of the adults in college came from socioeconomic groups similar to those of younger students. Until the mid-1980s, the return to learning in college settings was largely a middle-class phenomenon. Most of the adults were men and women who had fallen off the college track due to a youthful lack of motivation to study, family and economic crises, or lower career expectations.

The adults in employability programs may be different. They are frequently from families in which college was never a real option and continuing education was rarely possible. They are often older and from minority backgrounds. They may lack basic skills, and English may be their second language.

Those who did not grow up in a college-bound culture need more information about colleges and how they work and may need more support services than did previous adult students. The language of semesters and credits and grade point averages and prerequisites may be foreign to them, and they may lack family understanding and support for their new goals. Most colleges and universities are already responding creatively to the challenge of new students, and complaints about their unresponsiveness are often based more on myth than on reality.

LIMITED RANGE OF SERVICES

Many colleges restrict the range of services they offer as partners in the learning system. Businesses could use assistance in designing ways to tap their own sources of expertise, disseminate their wisdom through learning networks within the company, and apply the knowledge to solving pressing business problems. Businesses usually end up managing these processes themselves because colleges and universities do not view themselves as resources in establishing workplaces as learning environments.

Colleges and universities respond quite differently to the need for education and training for the workforce. They vary in their sense of mission, in their willingness and ability to work cooperatively in training ventures, and in their flexibility. Universities may or may not consider employability programs to be relevant to their role in the larger community. Small private colleges may leap at the chance to enlarge their student bodies or may turn aside, unwilling to alter their current modus operandi and culture by serving blue-collar workers.

Even community colleges cannot always be counted on for a positive response. Although the mission of two-year community colleges has generally been defined, at least in part, as providing vocationally oriented education and although community colleges have been in the forefront of service to nontraditional students, not all have embraced nontraditional methods and content or new forms of community service. Even in the vocational schools, where one might expect unlimited enthusiasm for the opportunity to become significant players in the nation's drive to train the workforce, the response has been mixed.

Similarly, a company's willingness to work with colleges and universities may be compromised by a lack of understanding of the contribution colleges can make in transforming work settings into learning environments.

The vocational education schools, which may have the most to gain from involvement in employability programs, are frequently slowest on the uptake. Participation in employability programs would spur them to update their curricula and might well provide the means to acquire new equipment and attract new faculty.

Although much of the training that occurs in employability programs is provided through community colleges, technical and vocational schools, and the adult basic skills programs of the public school systems, universities and four-year colleges also have an important role to play. The aspirations of many skilled workers, at both managerial and nonmanagerial levels, make them able candidates for advanced college or even graduate work. These students contribute a practical, experiential familiarity with specific business practices and technologies that allows them to grasp theoretical concepts more confidently than their inexperienced fellow students. If instructors capitalize on the presence of these older students, with the richness of their work backgrounds, they can enrich the classroom experience for everyone.

REWARDS OF COOPERATION

There are hundreds of examples across the country of partnerships with business, government, and labor organizations in which schools' faculty, libraries, research capability, curriculum, and instructional know-how are being put to fresh and innovative uses to train the American workforce.

Using existing education resources can be cost effective. It would be simpler and less expensive for Eureka Insurance Company to send three of its clerks to the local community college for a course in Lotus 1-2-3 spreadsheet management than to hire a consultant to teach a course and evaluate the results. What might cost about $525 in the community college could easily cost over $5,000 if done on-site on a one-time-only basis. Similarly, many laboratory-based or generic courses that do not require custom designing for company needs are more effectively delivered by education providers outside the company than by in-house training departments.

REQUIREMENTS FOR
SCHOOLS' SUCCESSFUL PARTICIPATION

CAEL's experience with employability programs suggests that institutions wishing to participate must be willing to introduce the full continuum of services outlined in this chapter, including availability of the expertise of faculty, access to all educational resources, and use of expertise on learning processes. Educational institutions must also contribute high-level administrative support, designate boundary spanners, provide adult-oriented services, support learners' transitions, be flexible about payment arrangements, recognize prior learning, and aim for a full range of services. These traits are discussed in the following paragraphs.

The top administration must thoroughly endorse employability programs. Their commitment should be evidenced by involvement in high-level discussions of contemplated programs and attendance at initial planning meetings. Programs that are bootlegged onto the campus by a few committed but powerless staff members cannot succeed over the long run.

The schools should designate administrators capable of performing as "boundary spanners" to link the campus and the outside world, smooth out the bureaucratic snarls that threaten success in their own organizations, and work with business, labor, or government agencies to overcome barriers and misunderstandings. Accomplished boundary spanners are comfortable with the different languages of the business, labor, and government worlds and can discern possibilities where others see only problems. They have a broad perspective on the multiple possibilities for cooperation and do not limit their thinking to the buying and selling of customized training or traditional college courses.

Schools should offer programs and student services that meet the needs of adult workers. Possible programs and services include:

■ Availability of administration and service offices, libraries, and classes in early mornings, late afternoons, evenings, and weekends;

■ Flexibility as to deadlines and test dates;

■ Special services for adults, such as career development or counseling, prematriculation academic advisement, basic skills workshops, and prior learning assessment programs;

- Practical and up-to-date course content, particularly in professional and technical areas;

- Financial aid for part-time older students; and

- Flexibility regarding instructional delivery systems and use of new technologies and nontraditional methods to stimulate learning and impart knowledge.

The school must be willing to have one or more counselors or administrators trained to serve as facilitators of a Returning to Learning® workshop (see Chapter 11) or some similar transitional activity and as counselors for worker-learners.

The school should be willing to accept tuition vouchers or other forms of noncash assurance as payment for instruction, to be redeemed by the sponsoring organization.

Schools wishing to serve working students should examine their own philosophies regarding the value of experiential learning students have already acquired through work, military service, hobbies, and interests. To what extent can potential students expect to have their learning tested and assessed for purposes of placement and credit awards under the school's present policies? Are the school's current practices adequate to serve this new population? Should they be revised in light of what has been learned about the process of assessment, its validity, its fairness, and its power as a means of recognizing individual accomplishment?

The ideal employability program would involve a geographically related group of postsecondary institutions providing a full range of services, from liberal arts, technical, and vocational courses to consultations on business issues and on the optimal ways of serving businesses' needs for education and training.

Figure 6.4 illustrates in simplified form the range of participation from minimal to ideal services. Partners might begin at the low end of the continuum and work their way toward more and more effective provisions.

Figure 6.4

REQUIREMENTS FOR SCHOOLS' PARTICIPATION IN EMPLOYABILITY PROGRAMS

Minimal	Ideal
■ Support from the top	■ Actual commitment from the top
■ Encouragement for boundary spanners	■ Assignment of boundary spanners
■ Provision of services for adult learners	■ Provision of work-to-school workshops & counseling services as needed
■ Limited flexibility in scheduling, content, delivery modes & methods of payment	■ Great flexibilty in scheduling, content, delivery modes, & methods of payment
■ Willingness to consider prior learning assessment credit in transfer	■ Willingness to offer a prior learning assessment program
■ Offering courses on-site to unions, corporations, & government groups	■ Engaging in full, consultative partnerships with unions, corporations, & government groups

---

This is a formidable series of potential adjustments. The Carnegie Council on Policy Studies in Higher Education (1980) highlighted universities' historical resistance to change.

"Taking, as a starting point, 1530, when the Lutheran Church was founded, some 66 institutions that existed then still exist today in the Western

World in recognizable forms: the Catholic Church, the Lutheran church, the parliaments of Iceland and the Isle of Man, and 62 universities. Universities in the past have been remarkable for their historic continuity, and we may expect this same characteristic in the future. They have experienced wars, revolutions, depressions, and industrial transformations, and have come out less changed than almost any other segment of their societies." (9)

With this long-standing tradition of resisting externally initiated change, it is to the colleges' great credit that so many of them have met the challenge.

WHAT SCHOOLS CAN GAIN FROM PARTICIPATING

Having addressed the adjustments schools must make to get onto the playing field, we can now look at how schools gain from playing (see Figure 6.1).

One immediate benefit is a greater influx of adult students. Most schools in the United States have already seen the concept of lifelong learning pay off in the return of substantial numbers of people "over college age" to campus. In 1990, the most recent update of figures on enrollments from the Department of Education showed that 60 percent of credit enrollments at undergraduate level in 1987 were adults at least 23 years old, and 42 percent were 25 or older. The number of undergraduates over age 25 more than doubled between 1972 and 1987, from 2.5 million to 5.2 million students (Goldberg 1990). These figures, though impressive, may represent a significant undercount because of the methodology used.

According to more reliable College Board data, the adult share of total annual college credit enrollment was at least 45 percent in 1987. By now it includes over 6 million adults and it continues to grow (College Board 1988). A more recent study done by the American Council on Education, with help from the National Center for Educational Statistics, sets the total 1987 postsecondary enrollment at over 18 million rather than 12.5 million, with the difference due largely to earlier underestimates of older adult enrollments.

In any case, these older, nontraditional students have eased the drop in enrollment that might have been expected as the baby-boom generation matured. These adults are a critical component of institutional economics. Moreover, it is universally acknowledged that they have brought a new dimension to campus life; it is no longer considered odd to see gray heads in front of the desk as well as behind it.

The increasing presence of adult students has significantly altered the nature and function of most community colleges. Already closely tied to their communities through state and local funding, these colleges are enhancing their ties to business, industry, and labor through a variety of special programs and relationships, on campus and off. Worker training projects of various kinds have sometimes been accompanied by corporations' donations of state-of-the-art equipment, part-time teaching by professionals in the field, and linkages with local public radio and television stations and cable companies to deliver instruction to the larger community. Examples of innovative, program-enhancing partnerships abound.

The most important prize for schools participating in employability programs is that they come to be perceived as a more integral part of their communities and as significant players in current affairs. This change can help a university embark on a dialogue with industry, labor, or government that can result in research partnerships, shared resources, technology transfer programs, consulting relationships, and faculty sabbaticals as scientific advisors or managers in some companies.

New students, financial rewards, enhanced resources, improved community stature, cooperative arrangements for knowledge and resource sharing, faculty and staff development opportunities — these are major "wins" that may draw even some of our more elite institutions into the network of employability programs.

CHAPTER

THE FEDERAL & STATE
GOVERNMENTS AS PARTNERS

The burdensome federal deficit, the enormous international trade deficit, and the current losses of jobs and enterprises to competitors from abroad suggest that the United States is in economic decline. While assuring a productive workforce is by itself no guarantee against decline, it is a precondition of other measures. These include protection of a full supply of American jobs, exploitation of new technologies to achieve high efficiencies in production, reduction of the unfavorable balances of trade, and mastery of the federal and state deficits. The question we address in this chapter, then, is: How can state and federal governments provide a context congenial to human resource development? What programs and policies can they enact to further this end and thereby bolster the U.S. economy?

Both the federal and state governments are essential partners in achieving employability and profitability in the American economy. Governments act in four complementary ways: *"They permit. They encourage. They direct. They forbid"* (Thomas 1991). With respect to each of these four types of action, the federal government and the states "divide the labor," and ideally complement one another in doing so.

These are exactly the kinds of actions that President Bush and the governors were choosing as they determined the goals to be achieved in the educational system by the year 2000. To illustrate the application of the four powers to employability issues, Congress might pass bills *permitting* welfare recipients to receive college tuition scholarships as nontaxable income or *encouraging* states to experiment with employability programs. The federal government might further *direct* that every employer must either spend 1.5 percent of payroll on an employability program of its own choice or pay that amount into a state fund that would be used collectively to enhance employability in that state. The Congress might further *forbid* that colleges spend a disproportionate share of federal aid (earned by virtue of older adult part-time enrollments) on their younger, full-time students. The states might complement these federal actions by *encouraging* collaborative planning by industry groups or at the county or city level among small businesses with incentive funding.

Before we explore the questions such ideas raise about the relationships among the learning system, employability, and competitiveness, let us first bear in mind what the society and its governing entities stand to gain by acting prudently on these issues.

HOW THE STATES & THE NATION BENEFIT

Why were state governors from South Carolina, Tennessee, Indiana, New York, Arkansas, and Georgia among the most active leaders of efforts in 1990 to generate an employable and ever more productive workforce? The answer is straightforward. These governors wanted to enhance the financial capacity of their states.

By acting as a catalyst to upgrade the productivity of the workforce, a state gains more jobs with higher wages, a higher level of economic activity, a better mix of economic enterprises, and a growing tax base. In addition, a state committed to active partnerships in an employability program can increase services to the state's highest taxpayers — business and industry — and thereby woo continuing support. An exemplary employability program can also attract additional industries from other states.[1] These generative benefits help to maximize a state's revenues.

The mitigative benefits of a productive workforce include alleviating poverty, structural unemployment, and public assistance. A more employable and productive workforce lowers rates and costs of unemployment, volume and costs of people on welfare, incidence of delinquency and crime, and volume and costs of unfunded health and medical coverage.

A statewide program of employee growth and development will not be a cure-all for these ills, but it will reliably contribute to reducing their economic and social costs. Moreover, the benefits will accumulate with time. So the costs of funding the employability effort can legitimately be viewed as a capital outlay in its beginning years and also as a way to reduce the rise of net costs of state and federal services.

In short, what can be gained from a strategy to produce an ever better-qualified workforce is economic strength and prosperity for the country as a whole. What the government per se gains (tax revenues, lowered downside costs, etc.) will be, relatively speaking, a side benefit. Figure 7.1 summarizes how governments help and benefit from employability programs.

THE CONTEXT FOR NATIONAL GAINS

To grasp the broader context as to what the federal government might best permit, encourage, direct, and forbid, consider briefly the arena of global competition.

The federal government seeks means that do not cause one state to prosper at the expense of others. States do not deliberately set out to harm one another, but when push comes to shove, individual states put their own short-run interests ahead of the

---

1. This benefit is good for the receiving state but bad for others. The federal government must either mediate competition among states (as it does in regulating interstate commerce) or help governors negotiate a framework for reducing such downside side effects.

long-term general welfare. Only a firmly enforced compact can prevent such developments.

Figure 7.1

HOW GOVERNMENTS HELP & BENEFIT IN EMPLOYABILITY PROGRAMS

What Is the Idea?

- A productive workforce is a key factor in a prosperous economy.

- State (or province) & federal governments can provide incentives to employers & education providers to invest in employability.

- A more prosperous economy yields higher tax base and lower costs for the remediation of social ills.

How Governments Help & Benefit

How They Help	How They Benefit
■ Refrain from taxing education benefits to worker or employer	■ Lower unemployment costs
	■ Lower welfare costs
■ Require educational providers to recognize prior learning with credit & advanced standing	■ Lower costs of social services related to poverty & crime
■ Mandate an integrated system of recognition of credentials	■ Better educated citizenry
	■ More prosperous economy
■ Provide re-employment assistance	■ Higher tax base & resulting revenues
■ Provide incentives for employer investment in employee growth & development programs	

The U.S. government acts toward the governments of other peoples much as our states act toward one another. Just as short-sightedness among states may work against their collective long-term best interests, so it is with national governments. In the long run it is in the interests of all that the economies of others prosper, for if they do they will bring greater trade to one another. This means better markets for all.

Think of the world economic order as similar in certain key respects to the National Football League. The players (whether teams or national economies) must compete vigorously and honestly to allot the greatest benefits to fans (consumers in the economies). Who, after all, wants phony victories in football or false prosperity in an economy? Moreover, to make lucrative contracts with the telecommunications industry to broadcast their games, the members of the league work together to get a good deal. (The lucrative contracts in world trade are the expanded markets that economic development of all nations can elicit.) Because many contestants will languish if the game is not played fairly, competition must be controlled and regulated by a system in which all cooperate to establish and enforce rules (stating what is permitted, encouraged, forbidden, and directed) that define the game and ensure fair play. The point is that cooperation must govern the competition, and the competition must be genuine and vigorous.

In a world economy, unlike the NFL, it is not intended that there be a champion each year who competes to be the best. On the contrary, the great boon of a sound world economy, as of world friendship, is that every country can do better than before and be best in its own economic niches.

Niches, to complicate matters, never seem to stay put. The United States was once the leading textile manufacturer and exporter in the world. The Japanese took over much of the textile field from the United States in the mid-century. But now they've lost most of it to Korea, China, and other developing economies. Is the same thing about to happen to Japan with automobiles? Electronics?

This is not the place, nor are we the people, to say what particular niches the United States is best positioned to seek in the world economy. The point is that competition among national economies must be conducted not as a war among adversaries but as a game among partners in a fairly conceived and regulated competition to serve the goals of employability for workers and profitability for enterprises. Attempts by one nation or a set of nations to control the outcome of the competition or even the course of play, beyond establishing and enforcing rules of fair competition, can have seriously adverse effects. We have seen this on a lesser scale in the centralized control of production and distribution in the Eastern European economies. The United States stands to gain, within such a system of fair play, ongoing economic health, stabilizing political influence, a gradually improving standard of living, the social well-being of its people and, last but not least, near universal employability.

ACTIONS TO UNDO

Before turning to the ways governments may promote employability, let us look briefly at the record of recent government actions. Ironically, the federal government has instituted some 42 measures that *prevent* or *hinder* adults from pursuing the learning they need to qualify for steady or higher-paying jobs or to make themselves into better citizens. These measures range from denying access to education for those on welfare to making child care unaffordable for those trying to escape poverty through training.

Each of these 42 policies or practices was enacted for good reasons. The remedy, in each case, is not to undo the measure entirely, but to amend it to preserve its original purpose while avoiding its adverse side effects on adult learning and worker productivity (Gold 1990).

Student Financial Assistance:

When Thomas's framework for understanding governmental actions is applied to student financial assistance policies, the clumsiness of government's attempts is apparent. Many governmental directives are inappropriate or counterproductive. In practice, these notions are obstacles to worker-learners: 1) the definition of base-year income (a way to see that the student and his or her family contribute a fair share); 2) the practical ineligibility of some less than half-time learners for aid; 3) the failure of colleges to provide a proportionate share of available aid to needy part-time students; 4) the failure of need calculations to distinguish between financial demands on low-income heads of household and unmarried younger students; 5) artificially low allowances for day-care costs for Pell grant aid recipients; 6) states counting nontuition federal aid as lowering the recipient's eligibility for welfare and food stamps; and 7) the inaccessibility of financial aid information to part-time and evening students. Governmental prohibitions have similar unintended impact — for example, the ineligibility of less than half-time students for Perkins or Stafford loans.

Unemployment Insurance:

In many states, recipients of unemployment insurance are routinely suspected of trying to evade work if they seek education and training to qualify for better, more sustained work opportunities. Claimants are not informed of their options and rights to pursue education suited to their most appropriate employment.

Welfare:

Local caseworkers typically advise welfare recipients that postsecondary education is not an allowable training activity for them and that they cannot continue to receive welfare benefits unless they abandon college for a menial job or for some short-term training opportunity. Also, since federal financial aid in excess of tuition and fees is normally counted as income, it reduces welfare eligibility. These two practices, now permitted or even encouraged, should be forbidden by changes in federal law, with follow-up on implementation.

Food Stamps:

At present an adult seeking to attend college is required to work at least 20 hours a week, no matter how many courses he or she is taking, and may not deduct educational expenses from income in applying for food stamps.

Vocational Rehabilitation:

State and local caseworkers often discourage or prevent recipients of vocational rehabilitation benefits from attending postsecondary education in any form, especially if the recipients have severe handicaps.

Dependent Care:

Federal laws do not support accessible, affordable day-care options for enough working adults to allow the U.S. to reach its employment goal. In addition, federal policy makes it difficult to count the costs of child care accurately in assessing parents' need and eligibility for federal aid.

Employee Education Benefits:

In 1978 Congress ruled that education benefits provided by the employer were not subject to taxation as ordinary income. The 1978 provision (Section 127 of the tax code [P.L. 95-600]) was extended for five years and has been renewed ever since. But the extension always runs out before it is renewed, and then the renewal is made retroactive. This pattern has had a measurably chilling effect on employee participation. For example, the UAW-GM employee growth and development program experienced a major drop in participation the last time this pattern was repeated.

In addition, the latest extension limited benefits in dollar value and ruled out the exemption for costs of some kinds of education important to a highly qualified workforce. Contrary to government's claim, the overwhelming proportion of workers affected are nonmanagement employees (Coopers and Lybrand 1989, cited in Gold 1990). A different set of actions is required to avoid a severe disincentive to both employers and employees.

Adult Education:

For adults who lack basic learning skills or who have not completed high school, the key federal provision for help is the Adult Education Act. There is a need for more adequate information on the relative effectiveness of different education providers and for follow-up action to make greater use of the most cost-effective providers.

Vocational-Technical Education:

The Carl Perkins Act of 1984, as amended, is today's primary source of federal support for vocational education. Here, as in the case of federal support for adult education, there is a serious lack of consensus about how best to use the funds and a lack of adequate studies to support a sound conclusion.

The Job Training Partnership Act:

There is a sense in the postsecondary education community that the Job Training Partnership Act, created to help disadvantaged youth and adults find permanent self-sustaining employment, is administered in a way that discourages colleges' participation. Performance standards are needed that take account of the need for longer-term training options for unemployed people with potential for more demanding work roles (Gold 1990). For example, training for accountants requires more time than training for bookkeepers but also offers greater employment security. For applicants with the potential, longer training is normally a superior investment of public and private money.

ACTIONS TO TAKE

Undoing directives and prohibitions that adversely affect adults' return to learning could help the cause of productivity substantially. But much more is needed. We suggest a shared leadership role for federal and state governments and a division of labor among them and the other key partners. (See Chapter 13 for details on how government could provide proactive leadership.) We begin with a discussion of the incentives government can provide for employed workers.

INCENTIVES FOR EMPLOYED WORKERS

Hundreds of major corporations already have in place a tuition-assistance program. For their currently employed workers, modest additional state incentives or subsidies could strengthen these programs to multiply the participation rates by five to twenty times. Here are some examples of incentives a state might offer:

1. Refrain from taxing the dollar value of education and training benefits as current income to the employee. Taxing these benefits lowers participation, lowering the net gain to the state from employees' giving their own time and from corporations' paying the costs of their keeping qualified for changing jobs.

2. Use a funding formula for public education institutions serving worker-learners that does not penalize an institution for accepting these learners. Better yet, reward the successful provider institution with additional financial support (e.g., by partial funding on a basis other than full-time equivalency of enrollments).

3. Allow employers a modest tax credit on the increase of their expenditures for training and educating their workers in generic skills, capabilities, and knowledge.

4. Provide for worker-learners a brokering and career advising support service comparable to the EGDPs described in chapters 4 and 5.

5. Adopt a market-oriented system among the education providers. Monitor the quality of the providers' services and achievements to guarantee that workers get their money's worth.

6. Mandate that worker-learners not be required to pay tuition money for, or spend time repeating, what they already know and can do. Establish a unitary statewide credential-recording and credential-retrieval service to enforce the requirement that learning costs not be duplicated.

7. Create partnerships such as those currently at work in Connecticut, in which the Departments of Labor and Economic Development, the University of Connecticut, and a business cooperate to develop manufacturing sites as learning environments.

8. Provide opportunities for paid educational leave. This option is popular in Europe, where the government provides a tax benefit to corporations or to individuals for money invested in an educational account. This option has also been used in some Canadian provinces and may be enhanced by federal incentives, as the Canadian example suggests.

This is only an illustrative list. The costs of these measures need not be prohibitive. In fact, a number of states are already using them. Clearly, the federal government could cooperate in assisting states with funding such incentive systems or with other incentives to leverage state action.

Even stronger measures have already been used in some countries to encourage recurrent worker education. France has an employee training tax of some 1.5 percent of the payroll. Employers can partially or wholly avoid it if, on their own initiative and at their own expense, they provide appropriate training or education for updating and enhancing the qualifications and credentials of their workforce. In Sweden there are substantial state subsidies for training and educating adults through the formal education system, making possible low or no tuition charges. In the United States, public subsidies of community colleges, undergraduate four-year degree programs, and public universities have a similar effect.

INCENTIVES FOR UNEMPLOYED WORKERS

A number of obstacles contribute to the nonparticipation of many potential workers in the current workforce. Consider the following ways government can help unemployed workers overcome obstacles to their employability.

1. Provisions for child care, either by the employer or by the municipality or the state, can remove one obstacle that keeps a single parent from work. If the job pays sufficiently good wages, the formerly unemployed person can pay for child care provided at a sufficiently low cost. Even in two-parent families, with both parents able and eager to work, child care may be a crucial determinant as to whether both remain optimally employed.

2. Many of the unemployed are on welfare benefits, which they lose automatically under current state laws when they take a job. If the job is a low-paying one and health benefits provided on welfare are also lost, the potential worker may be better off on welfare. Governments can remove this obstacle by revising the welfare laws and regulations to enable a prospective worker to make a net gain in economic condition when shifting from welfare to work.

3. An inability to pay for tuition, books, fees, and related education costs is a real obstacle to employability. Even employed workers have a hard time meeting the costs of education, and they may have an employer or union (or both) willing to pay at least part of these costs. A state that wants to reduce the burden of welfare and related costs by getting unemployed

workers without financial reserves back into the workforce must view these education costs as a capital investment.

4. Underestimating potential — for productive work and for earnings as well as for learning — is one of the most common obstacles to workers' keeping up their qualifications. It can be a sentence of permanent dependency. Often the underestimate is not just the opinion of observers, but shared by the unemployed person. Most individuals cannot overcome these attitudes without assistance from others (Cross 1981). A state might help by providing support counseling or organizing support groups. An even simpler solution is to engage learners with low self-esteem in a successful, short-term educational experience. According to Cross, successful participation in a learning experience is the most powerful way to alter disabling internalized barriers to learning.

5. State governments also have laws, regulations, and common practices that discourage learning and employability through ill-conceived efforts to achieve other worthy purposes.

6. Imprisonment, drug addiction, and delinquency are all obstacles to employability. A number of potentially employable people, who by becoming steady workers could greatly enhance their lives, are prevented from doing so because they are confined for criminal behavior or locked in a disabling addiction to drugs or to some form of antisocial behavior. The causes of their problems are legion, as is the number of solutions. But if a state adopted the policy that for every such person within its jurisdiction there had to be a plan of rehabilitation and re-employment, and if it assigned responsibility for achieving this plan, current outlays and efforts would have a greater chance of success.

7. A number of otherwise employable people are disabled by poor health. The failure of state and federal governments to provide an effective safety net for restoring the curable and treatable ill to a condition of employability has to be counted as one of the causes of the high net cost of unemployment.

SETTING AN EXAMPLE

Some government agencies have entered into modest employability programs on behalf of their own employees. For example, the U.S. Department of Agriculture is said to operate one of the largest educational institutions in the country. Similarly, many states conduct extensive in-service programs on topics from word processing and database management to supervision and management training.

But employability programs are rare within government. Its education and training benefits, like most in the corporate world, are posited upon immediate applicability of the training to its employees' current jobs. If the governor and the legislature see the type of employability programs defined here as desirable for business and are ready to support them, why not lend more credibility to their position by setting up a kindred employability program for their own employees?

Since 1990 CAEL has been working with Indiana, Ohio, New York, and Georgia to develop their own approaches and mechanisms for workforce development. With support from the W. K. Kellogg Foundation and the Joyce Foundation, and with matching support from the states themselves, these four states have chosen different paths toward creating a climate that encourages employability.

Beginning with a Governor's Summit on Workforce Development, which brought government, business, labor, and civic leaders together, Indiana has worked at state and local levels to develop employability services for its steel industry (among others) and to enhance the state Department of Education and Training Services to improve its assessment and placement services. A statewide plan for workforce development is being created to offer Indiana workers universal access to the training and education needed to assure their employability. With the establishment of a Training 2000 Fund, the state has begun to assist both small and large businesses and to invest in raising the level of the workforce's transferable skills.

In Ohio, initial efforts have moved toward expanding CAEL's existing joint ventures into diverse industries. In New York, CAEL has been training partner agencies to take on its role in stimulating joint-venture activity regionally. In Georgia, through a partnership led by the University of Georgia, the post-secondary educational community is seeking business and government cooperation in employee development.

On its own initiative, the Connecticut Department of Labor sought to expand its services by helping manufacturing companies adopt innovative practices. During the first planning meetings, the response from manufacturers was quite pointed: *"Show us first that you can practice what you preach. Can a state agency show us how to innovate?"* In response, the Department of Labor initiated a major reorganization of the employment insurance and job service functions.

One activity, particularly relevant to this book, was the approach to requests for improved training services. Overall, manufacturers were unhappy with the education and training system offered by the state. Rather than provide more of the same, the Department of Labor established a partnership with the University of Connecticut to help businesses maximize the learning potentials of the workplace. Three corporations participated in the pilot effort. In each case the Department of Labor, the university, and the corporation each assumed a third of the program cost. Details on this project are in Chapter 12.

These five instances of state-based initiatives in workforce development illustrate the enormous potential of state leadership in accomplishing the goal of universal employability.

BUILDING BLOCKS OF A NATIONWIDE EMPLOYABILITY PROGRAM

An economy cannot move goods and people rapidly enough to be competitive today without an elaborate, first-rate infrastructure of roads, rails, airports, and regulatory and facilitative services provided by the federal and state governments. Just as contemporary transportation requires an infrastructure, so do employability and competitiveness of enterprise. While neither the federal government nor the state governments can pay for or do everything necessary to create and maintain the employability infrastructure, their leadership, coordination, regulatory services, and facilitative participation are essential to its existence. Clearly all essential partners must play their roles, but without political support and systematization the nongovernmental partners cannot bring about a system that will optimize the performance of all workers and the varieties of businesses from the largest to the smallest.

Of what does such an infrastructure consist? Consider the analogy of a construction project. A viable construction project is made up not just of building blocks but also of connecting and supporting members that fit into a coherent whole and make it work as intended. If the blocks are not tied together within a sound design, the project will be either just a pile of blocks, a structure that will collapse under the first major strain, or at best a structure that does not do what it is meant to do. In the case of the U.S. economy, we have been better at creating good building blocks than creating a design for their assembly into a solid, effective whole.

We do not presume to lay out a blueprint for the entire array of provisions required for a national employability program. What we propose here are an overview and clarification of the major features of the needed structures and activities and a discussion of which parts are in place, which are yet to be created, and how they would interact. The following eight building blocks are essential to a successful employability program.

Education & Training Institutions:

One of the most important tools required is the talent and facilities to staff and carry out the education and training needed. We have this tool in hand. If we commit to responding to societal needs for universal employability, it could be our most valuable resource and foundation for the infrastructure.

A Viable Economy:

A second major building block is a functioning economy with only a modest level of unemployment and a tolerable proportion of chronically unemployed. At the moment a major concern is with those who are not chronically unemployed and yet cannot find work that makes use of their capabilities. This building block also includes a large array of quite diverse enterprises, from very large to very small and in every area of economic production and service.

A Workforce with the Potential
to Achieve the Needed Array of Qualifications:

There are countries whose populace is impoverished, illiterate, and in other ways severely handicapped in the potential for reaching qualifications needed for a globally competitive workforce. In contrast, although the U.S. workforce falls considerably short of being ideally qualified, its potential is high. (See Chapter 8.)

A Brokering-Managing Cadre for Employability Services:

A fourth building block that is partially in place is a small component of broker-managers for employability programs. CAEL is, to the best of our knowledge, the largest and most successful of the neutral, third-party broker-managers currently at work. There appear also to be the beginnings of much larger service providers in this area.

At present, then, is a small model element, including both broker-managers for Fortune 500 corporations and a few examples of broker-managers for coalitions of small businesses. Some colleges and collegiate consortia are offering elements of these services locally, though they may be brokering only their own services. Missing is the overwhelming volume of such providers that will eventually be needed.

A Financing & Financial Aid System:

This fifth essential building block of employability and productivity is partially in place. As described in Chapter 6, there is a large outlay per year for worker training and education. We estimate that the pace of growth of knowledge and technology calls for a new level of worker training and education. When compounded with the general backlog of unmet training needs and the pervasive, long-standing problem of undertraining, this adds up to a need for an annual investment double to triple the current level. One way to check this estimate is to ask, *"What increase in worker participation in education and training is needed to meet the demands in worker qualification of a truly competitive economy?"* CAEL's experience with EGDPs indicates that participation may triple where appropriate financing, advocacy, support services, and networking occur.

Ideally, financing should cover both the tuition and learning costs involved and the costs of brokering and managing projects and coordinating partners. We believe such financing will not be achievable on a national scale and in a way that serves small as well as large businesses without statewide and nationwide advocacy, regulatory, and incentive systems.

Advocacy Institutions:

Another building block, partially in place, is that of effective advocacy for workers with respect to their education and training needs. Interestingly, forward-looking corporations have played a major role in this advocacy thus far. Most of them have done so, however, strictly in terms of stronger education and training efforts in-house. Only a few leading unions now accord high priority to this need. A few governmental and unaligned nonprofit voices can be heard. But most members of the workforce are still without effective advocacy.

Research & Technical Services:

An organization called Jobs for the Future exemplifies a component of an adequate national employability system: ongoing research and technical services that enable the essential partners, including state governments, to know what jobs are needed, how the area's supply of workers fits its needs, and how the education and training offerings fit employee development needs. Numerous research efforts of a broader nature exist, but they are not harnessed to a coherent body of national goals and policy. The capability is present, but it is not being used to facilitate a coherent employability program.

Public Policy & Implementing Agencies:

A final element essential to a nationally effective employability program, but only partially in place, is state and governmental policies that stimulate investment in employability, support parts of a comprehensive employability program that cannot or will not be paid for by employers and workers, and provide a regulatory framework within which the needed workforce development can occur efficiently. Parts of such a pattern of policies and structure are in place. But, as shown in Chapter 6 and the earlier part of this chapter, they are seriously inadequate to the scale and nature of the problems to be addressed.

UPGRADING THE WORKFORCE

PART 3

addresses the task of enabling workers to keep up with the demand for ever-changing job qualifications.

Chapter 8

outlines the qualifications workers will need, noting a substantial mismatch between their present skills and those needed for ongoing employability.

Chapter 9

discusses how workers can close the skills gap. Essentially five paths are available: from high school to work, from college to work, from work to school, from welfare to work and school, and by transforming work into school. The chapter then estimates the scope of effort required of workers to close their gap and of education and training providers to serve the workers' needs.

Chapter 9 also argues for a new credentialing system that establishes a common currency for skills, knowledge, and experience that can be used by workers, employers, unions, and educators alike.

Finally, Chapter 10

addresses the thorny question of whether programs designed to upgrade the workforce can be mounted without worsening the competitive situation of currently disadvantaged people — including those who are undereducated, poorly paid or unemployed, or suffering discrimination that impedes their chances of supporting themselves and their families or of advancing in their careers.

THE SKILLS EMPLOYERS SEEK & EMPLOYEES NEED

Employability, as noted in Chapter 1, means being qualified for currently available work. As William Brock, former secretary of labor in the Reagan administration, said, *"The good news is that American employers are largely satisfied with the skills of the American workforce. And the bad news is that American employers are largely satisfied with the skills of the American workforce"* (1990). Brock went on to explain that American business, rather than responding to the challenges of the world economy by reorganizing work for greater productivity, which would demand greater skills, has more frequently deskilled jobs to match the skill levels of immediately available workers. By demanding less instead of more, American business is using the competitive strategy employed by Third World countries. A more advantageous approach would be to adopt the higher skill strategy used by more developed countries like Japan and Germany. As Ray Marshall, secretary of labor in the Carter administration, said about educating the workforce, *"The best way to fail today is to do what we did well yesterday"* (cited in Brock 1990). By August of 1993 many large employers were downsizing their workforces, reducing waste in the use of manpower, but not necessarily reorganizing work to make best use of more highly skilled labor. This chapter expands and clarifies our discussion of the skills the workforce needs.

It is old news that American workers today have major skill deficiencies. Although other advanced nations have programs of vocational education that are responsive to current skill needs, in the United States vocational education and secondary education systems are in serious disarray, as detailed in Chapter 6.

In Chapter 4, we noted that the management orientation of American companies may be more to blame than the skill deficiencies of individual workers, who in large part have the potential to attain the skills desired if they are encouraged and given the means to do so. In other developed nations, planners and educators start with the assumption that highly skilled, highly productive workers are necessary to their economies; here we accept an abysmally low standard of "getting by." For example, 50 percent of our high-school graduates cannot read above eighth-grade level or do eighth-grade mathematics. In an international algebra test for 17-year-olds from 12 countries, Japan came in highest, followed by Finland, the United Kingdom, Belgium, Israel, and Sweden; the U.S. came in last, slightly below Hungary (NCEE 1990, 43). We blush for this low performance and publicly lament the way we lag behind the other industrialized nations in workforce development, but we have not yet determined, as a nation, to put forth the will, the energy, and the resources that could change this situation.

As the need to increase our productivity forces this country to get on with the technological and structural workplace readjustments that will keep us competitive, untrained and unskilled workers will be the first casualties. They will be unable to move from their present jobs to different jobs at comparable pay. Many of them will become part of the working poor or the permanently unemployed.

LIFELONG LEARNING AS A REALITY

Education for employability has no defined beginning or end. Human learning begins in the cradle and ends in the grave. We begin to acquire the skills of communicating, working together, being flexible, and being adaptable long before we enter a formal school situation or work site. These skills continue to develop long after formal schooling ends. The exigencies of adult life frequently do not allow formal education to proceed in a linear fashion for extended periods of time. When formal study is undertaken by adults, it is often interrupted by demands of job, family, or work. Yet even so informal experiential learning continues (e.g., Candy 1991, Tough 1979).

Thus a key principle of employee growth and development programs is that they should foster a continuum of learning. A person encouraged by financial and programmatic support to return to learning in a formal sense was probably learning before the program began and will certainly continue to learn after it ends.

WHAT EMPLOYERS SAY THEY WANT

Many employers are not satisfied with the skills and competencies of the current workforce. They have serious reservations about maintaining productivity over the long haul with either their present employees or those coming into the workforce in the 1990s. Such employers express their needs in value-laden terms. They speak of developing a "work ethic," which usually includes attitudes like the following:

- Coming to work regularly and on time;
- Dressing appropriately and maintaining good grooming;
- Projecting a positive attitude;
- Sticking with the job;
- Doing one's best;
- Perceiving work as important;
- Treating one's employer and fellow workers with respect;
- Giving good value for wages; and
- Committing to the company's goals.

Employers also want to hire people who can express themselves clearly and can handle basic mathematical functions. They want people who can relate positively to clients or customers as well as to their co-workers, work well in groups, show evidence of the ability to "think on their feet," solve problems, and learn new skills and competencies.

This last quality, the ability to learn, is crucial. Business leaders, merchants, and factory owners are united in saying that if they can hire reasonably literate people who can think clearly and know how to learn, they will gladly forgo demanding specific vocational skills.[1] If people are capable of learning, they can be trained on the job in professional and technical skills.

WHAT EMPLOYEES SAY THEY WANT

What employees think they need in the way of skills and competencies is murkier. Few employees have been polled on this question. If, however, we can assume that they are voting by their choice of courses under nonrestricted, prepaid tuition programs, then we must conclude that their tastes are omnivorous, from theology to accounting, from computer science to the American novel. They choose primarily on the basis of their subject interests rather than the skills and competencies they will gain. This pattern can be expected, given the fact that course catalogs and college requirements are commonly stated in terms of content rather than competencies. The only language available to influence the learner's choice is that of the discipline itself.

If you ask individuals why they want to go back to school, however, their answers are expressed more in terms of competency. "I want to learn how to run my own business." "I want to be able to win arguments about politics with my wife's relatives." "I want to keep up with my kids in computers." "I want to understand how we can get rid of the pollutants that are messing up the

---

1. An internal paradox exists in the hiring and promotion practices of many corporations. Workers need specific abilities to get hired for a narrowly defined job. Once hired, these same employees require generic capabilities to get promoted.

streams and rivers where I used to fish." "I need to know how to get along better with people so that I can apply for a management job before the next layoffs." These adults may not have the vocabulary to discuss broad-based competencies in abstract terms, such as "accurate empathy," "influence skills," "persistence against obstacles," "drive for efficiency," and "ability to apply a general idea to a new problem." But these concepts are clearly embedded in what they say.

A CONSENSUS ON NECESSARY SKILLS

We are beginning to see a surprising amount of agreement on those skills and competencies that define someone as "employable," and the broad outlines of an employability curriculum are becoming clearer. Figure 8.1 outlines the commonalties among basic employability skills and competencies as described by five different groups: the American Society for Training and Development (ASTD), an organization that is particularly responsive to the needs and interests of business and industry; the Commission on the Skills of the American Workforce, a task force that is responding to a broad-based agenda of economic and labor development needs; American College Testing (ACT), an organization serving higher education and now developing Work Keys designed to assess the skills of individuals and to guide training efforts to develop skills matching the requirements of job groups; the U.S. Secretary of Labor's Commission on Achieving Necessary Skills (SCANS), a commission charged with providing guidance for improving the preparation of American workers; and German vocational education (as described in a 1990 report by Ute Laur-Ernst).

There is striking similarity among these five lists in the emphasis on effective use of resources, interpersonal skills, acquisition and use of information, understanding of organizational systems, and ability to work with a variety of technologies. The listings of skills provided by ACT, ASTD, and the Commission on

Figure 8.1

SKILLS NEEDED BY THE AMERICAN WORK FORCE

ASTD	Commission on Skills of the American Workforce	German Vocational Education	ACT	SCANS
Knowing how to learn	Capacity to learn, knowledge of high school subjects	Intellectual abilities	Ability to learn	Acquiring & evaluating information
Competence: reading, writing, computation	Reading, writing, computation		Reading, writing, computation	Basic skills
Communication: listening & oral communication		Communication	Listening & oral communication	Communicating information using a variety of technologies, negotiating
Adaptability: creative thinking, problem solving	Thinking, problem solving	Systems thinking	Problem solving, critical & scientific reasoning	Organizing, maintaining, & interpreting information
Personal management: self-esteem, goal setting, personal & career development	Ability to work alone	Personal development, emotional abilities, creativity, autonomy	Motivation & self-development	
Group effectiveness: interpersonal skills, negotiating skills, teamwork	Ability to work effectively in small groups	Social abilities, cooperation	Interpersonal skills, negotiation, teamwork	Understanding complex social, organizational, technical interrelationships; participating as team members
Influence: organizational effectiveness, leadership		Decision-making, planning, organizing	Organizational effectiveness, leadership	Ability to identify, organize, plan & allocate resources

the Skills of the American Workforce have strong similarities, perhaps because of their common use of the research base provided by Anthony P. Carnevale and his colleagues at ASTD (1990). These three reports all stress the following abilities: knowing how to learn; reading, writing, and computational competence; communication skills; problem-solving abilities; personal motivation and self-development capabilities; interpersonal skills; and leadership abilities. The German vocational education perspective adds to this list the ability to engage in systems thinking as well as decision-making, planning, and organizing abilities. The SCANS report supplements the list of skills with an emphasis on the ability to acquire and use information.

While the skills listed in Figure 8.1 are not the final word on this subject, they do reflect a remarkable agreement among educators, government, employers, and other commentators on what skills are necessary. If American workers are to remain employable, we must make available means for their acquiring and sustaining these skills.

KNOWING HOW TO LEARN

Without the ability to learn, workers will not use the opportunities to learn that are available in the workplace. The full use of those opportunities is essential to optimal productivity. Learning includes absorbing, processing, and applying new information. In addition to acquiring the basic skills necessary to learn, knowing how to learn includes becoming aware of one's own learning styles and preferences. It also means acquiring useful learning strategies to integrate those preferences for use in the task at hand.

BASIC ACADEMIC SKILLS: READING, WRITING, & COMPUTATION

Because of the increasing emphasis on information processing in today's jobs, reading, writing and computational skills are essential for employability. Reading tasks on the job are different from those encountered in classroom or leisure settings. *"They require the reader to be analytical, to summarize information, and to monitor [his or her] own comprehension of the reading task. This is an interpretive approach that requires the reader to have active involvement with the reading task. From the employer's perspective, basic training in reading should focus on teaching reading processes for locating information and for using higher level thinking strategies to solve problems"* (Carnevale, Gainer, and Meltzer 1990, 10).

Similarly, numerical literacy includes not only basic functions of arithmetic, algebra, geometry, trigonometry, and statistics but also familiarity with mathematical thinking, which is crucial in dealing with science and technology.

COMMUNICATIONS

Communication skills involve interacting with other people. They include oral skills such as speaking and listening as well as body language. But they also include computer literacy and familiarity with a variety of audio and visual media. Communications skills are tied to personal and professional development. They are especially crucial in the service industries, where acquiring and keeping clients and customers are central to achieving competitiveness.

COGNITIVE SKILLS

The development of thinking skills is receiving increased attention at every level of education. These capabilities form the basis for one's intellectual performance and include the ability to reason, evaluate, and solve problems. They also include the ability *"to synthesize information from prior analyses and diverse sources, the ability to understand many sides of a controversial issue, the ability to learn from experience"* (Chickering 1989, 137).

PERSONAL & CAREER DEVELOPMENT SKILLS

The competencies covered in this skill cluster are similar to aspects of the work ethic mentioned by employers. Self-esteem, motivation, and attention to one's personal and career goals are critical to understanding oneself in relation to work and behaving appropriately. Development of a positive self-image enables an employee to take pride in his or her work, to set goals, and to meet them. Carnevale, Gainer, and Meltzer (1990) observe that *"solid personal and career development skills are apparent in efficient integration of new technology or processes, creative thinking, high productivity, and a pursuit of skills enhancement through training or education. ... Self-esteem is at the core of training to expand job-specific occupational skills or provide remediation. ... From the shop floor to the salesroom, the motivated employee comes out on top"* (13).

INTERPERSONAL SKILLS & EFFECTIVENESS IN GROUPS

To some extent interpersonal skills come naturally to normal individuals, but to a large extent they are teachable. Interpersonal skills enable one to interact positively with people singly or in groups. In an era when teamwork is emphasized in the workplace, getting along with bosses and co-workers, pulling together for common goals, relating positively to clients and customers, tolerating different behaviors, and negotiating successfully are intimately tied to overall job performance.

ORGANIZATIONAL EFFECTIVENESS & LEADERSHIP

Carnevale, Gainer, and Meltzer (1990) define organizational effectiveness as *"an understanding of what organizations are, why they exist, and how one can navigate the complex social waters of varying types of organizations"* (15). Leadership, the ability to influence others' behavior and action, is bound up with organizational effectiveness as well as with a complex melding of interpersonal skills, clarity about personal and career development goals, the ability to communicate effectively, and self-esteem.

TRANSFERABILITY OF WORKPLACE SKILLS

Perhaps the most salient fact about all of these skills is that they are transferable. That is, they apply to a number of different job groups and functions. Transferability is, however, not automatic. Specific training in new arenas of application is often required. A good communicator can be trained to counsel drug abusers, lead a union, teach, or manage a production team. An adroit problem solver can solve problems in science, public relations, or management systems. To cite a more concrete example, suppose a job involves transferring numbers accurately from worksheets to a computer database in a factory setting. That skill will transfer easily to a job that demands similar accuracy, familiarity with numbers, and ability to use the computer in a laboratory, department store, or accounting office.

The generic nature of these skills has important implications for employability training. To teach a narrowly specific skill is to ensure that its lifespan is finite, dependent on changes in technology, changes in the way companies choose to structure work, and changes in the employee's circumstances and career goals. To teach a transferable skill is to ensure its usefulness in an ever-expanding number of jobs and life situations. Employability skills are truly "life skills." To achieve maximum flexibility and mobility, the workforce must have these broad-based transferable skills.

This is not to say that all training must be for transferable skills. Some training must address the specific skills needed today. For example, if a particular word-processing program is the overwhelming favorite of offices in a variety of companies, then it behooves a clerk who aspires to become a secretary to gain skill in that program. In this case, learning a narrow skill will not be detrimental because word-processing skills are themselves broadly transferable. One can go far more easily from Word Star to WordPerfect to Microsoft Word than from the typewriter to word processing in any program.

Readers can no doubt extract many examples of transferable and nontransferable skills from their own work experience. What is significant about transferable skills is that they go far beyond the mere learning of facts and data. They address the basis of all education, which is to teach people how to function in society, how to survive in a variety of situations, and how to retain the flexibility and ability to learn that are critical to achieving long-term employability.

It is important, finally, to see the overall place of the skills of the American workforce in the context of changes under way in the relative productivity of workers in competing countries. As Stewart (1992) reports, the average American worker, in spite of the competitive disadvantages mentioned earlier, produced in 1990 a higher dollar value of goods and services than any others in the world (after adjustment for purchasing power and for distortions derived from exchange rates). Labor flexibility (employers' options in hiring and firing, reorganizing, and deploying resources where most productive) is cited as the major cause of this result. But this productivity was improving more slowly than its rivals' and comparatively less well in the growing service sector than elsewhere. Only investing more in people and innovation, Stewart concludes, will make it possible to raise living standards in America.

EMPLOYABILITY SKILLS AS COGNITIVE PROCESSING

Is it pure happenstance that the consensus we report has emerged? Or is there a deeper basis for this analysis of the skills that make for employability? The employability skills just depicted are integral to *"mental self-management — the manner in which we order and make sense of events that take place around and within us"* (Sternberg 1988, p. x). The process of self-management that Sternberg calls "intelligence" involves a three-part structure: an adaptive part suiting behavior to context, an experiential part that applies ideas in practice, and a metacognitive part that clarifies purpose and strategies of coping.

The first part of mental self-management, the model tells us, is being able to fit behavior to a context. Contextually intelligent behavior involves (1) adapting to the present environment, (2) selecting a better environment, or (3) shaping the environment to make a better fit with one's skills, interests, and values. From this perspective, employability means simply knowing how to manage oneself in work contexts, using one or more of these three behaviors.

The second aspect of mental self-management is demonstrated when a person is (1) confronted with a relatively novel task or situation or (2) in the process of automating performance on a given task or in a given situation. This "experiential intelligence," as Sternberg calls it, is demonstrated by the ability to deal with new situations and to automate complex information-processing tasks (for example, reading or word processing). Once a person learns to use the computer, the next "intelligent" step is to make it an almost automatic habit. The more proficiently individuals can accomplish this task, the more employable they are.

The third aspect of intelligent behavior is the structures and mechanisms that underlie it. Sternberg says these fall into three sets: the executive, performance, and knowledge acquisition functions.

The executive functions include defining the problem that needs to be solved, deciding what categories of information to use in solving it, developing strategies to combine categories and information to solve it, deciding how to allocate resources (e.g., how much attention to pay to the problem), monitoring the solution, and remaining sensitive to external feedback. Notice how similar these tasks are to those outlined in Figure 8.1. A worker must learn to use these steps in a way appropriate to the particular job context. The worker must also be able to use them to adapt to novel situations in the workplace.

The performance functions of intelligence include (1) perceiving and storing new information, (2) putting together and comparing information, and (3) responding on the basis of available information. Workers who perform "intelligently" consistently utilize these three processes to enhance their behavior.

Finally, the knowledge acquisition components of intelligence include (1) sifting out relevant from irrelevant information, (2) combining selected information to form an integrated, plausible whole and (3) relating newly acquired or retrieved information to information acquired in the past. Workers who function "intelligently" acquire and apply information about their jobs and their performance by using these three processes.

The unawareness or lack of mastery of these elements of mental self-management and their interplay in work may be a fundamental difficulty with workers' ability to acquire and sustain high employability skills in today's world. This is a problem for workers as learners as well as for their teachers and supervisors. Efficiency in the workplace increasingly requires that everyone involved, from the top manager to the floor supervisor to the hands-on operator, possess the array of intelligent behaviors needed for the complex production tasks of contemporary technology. Understanding the nature of intelligent behavior in the work setting may be the most fundamental skill needed to enable workers to keep honing and developing working intelligence and thus employability.

Past interpretations of intelligence have treated it as a fixed, genetically determined quality. From this perspective, individuals (or groups of individuals) who have more of this prized quality are considered superior to individuals (or groups of individuals) who have less "intelligence." The authors do not adhere to this damaging line of thought. Sternberg's (1988) interpretation of intelligence is quite hopeful about human possibilities. He refers to the "capacity to develop capacity." In other words, individuals have the capacity to become more experientially, contextually, or metacognitively intelligent. If the partnerships outlined in Part 2 can collectively pool their resources, we as a country can significantly maximize individual workers' capacity to develop capacity.

CLOSING THE SKILLS GAP

The American economy has two unsolved problems in matching workers to employers' job requirements: not enough suitably qualified workers and poor information on the qualifications workers do have. We discuss in this chapter the transitions that workers use in trying to close the skills gap, the best arenas for doing so, and a way to document and share information on their skills to close the information gap.

In spite of the many resources and diverse providers available, large numbers of workers remain inadequately qualified for current and upcoming job requirements. For example, 70 percent of all high school seniors cannot write a basic letter seeking employment or correctly add their own lunch bills (Dole 1989). Fewer than one third of American 17-year-olds can solve math problems requiring several steps (Dertouzos, Lester, and Solow 1989). What can be done to address this problem?

Commissions and studies addressing "the reform of education" in the interest of the economy often focus on a single arena that is either their own turf or the one they perceive as most in need of development. Thus *A Nation at Risk* (1983), while basing its case for a better education system on the need for competitiveness, focused almost entirely on elementary and secondary schools, even though it was apparent that 80 percent of the workforce was already out of school and was for the most part in need of substantial upgrading (Dole 1989). Other studies have focused on what employers' own training programs can do to make up for what schools and colleges do not get done. Rarely have these studies spoken to the problems of transition into and out of school and work nor have they sought to understand how the system as a whole might function most effectively.

FIVE TRANSITIONS

To clarify the task of closing the skills gap, let us look at five kinds of transitions that would-be workers and currently employed workers face in trying to become and remain employable: the transitions from high school to work, from college to work, from work back to school, from welfare to school and work, and by transforming work into school. Our interest in this chapter is with facilitating workers' optimal use of education providers to achieve and maintain employability.

Transitions are never easy. Research studies (e.g., Schlossberg 1984) define transitions as events (like getting married) or nonevents (like not getting an expected promotion) that precipitate change. This research emphasizes that *adaptation* to the transition — not the transition itself — is the key. We should focus not on the loss of a job and related feelings but on how to adapt to the loss and get a new job. Factors affecting adaptation include the reason for the transition (is it a voluntary choice or imposed by an external agent?), the resources available during the transition (e.g., does the person have the time and energy to devote to adapting to the change?), and the nature of the post-transition environment (does it result in minor or major life-style changes?).

Passages from childhood to adolescence, from the single to the wedded state (and back again), aging, loss, and moves (emotional or geographic), all call for optimal human and institutional support systems to assist with adaptation. Transitions that have to do with moving from school to work, work to school, or welfare to work or school are frequently not recognized as demanding support. Better management of these critical transitions must be part of the effort to increase the employability of the American workforce.

FROM HIGH SCHOOL TO WORK

The school-to-work transition, although it comes close to being a universal experience, is frequently the most poorly managed of transitions. Indeed, *"America may have the worst school-to-work transition system of any advanced industrial country"* (NCEE 1990, 4).

American middle and high-school educators seem to believe that the major task of education is to prepare students for college. Yet data tell us that over 20 percent of students drop out of high school (in some New York City schools 80 percent of entering freshmen drop out before receiving a diploma), and that only about 50 percent of the remainder actually go on to enroll in college. So about 60 percent of young people go directly from school to work. Another 50 percent of those who do go on to college leave before earning a degree (Pascarella and Terenzini 1991). Thus, as many as 85 percent of our young people go from school (high school or college) to work without a diploma and only a fraction of them receive any substantial, sustained, technically current vocational, career, or personal counseling support in managing the transition.

Why do we ignore this important school-to-work transition? What can we do about the problem? Those high school students who do not intend to go on to college are all too often tracked into a watered-down academic curriculum rather than into one that combines academic with vocational studies focused on work-readiness skills and intelligent work behaviors (as defined in Chapter 8). In the past 50 years, vocational education has gotten increasingly short shrift in attention and funding, and the vocational curriculum in many states languishes with outdated curricula, equipment, and, sadly, teachers.

"Though high school vocational education has been supported by the federal government for over 70 years and enrolls over 5 million students annually, it has a very disappointing performance and is not generally viewed as a viable preemployment training system," write Dertouzos, Lester, and Solow (1989, 85). *"Employers do not see vocational high school programs as a prime source of skilled or even trainable workers. Indeed, often the fact of having participated in a vocational program stigmatizes workers in the eyes of employers."* The Commission on the Skills of the American Workforce (1990), deploring the lack of a coherent vocational program for many of those students who do not plan to go from high school to college, has called for a new approach to training the workforce of the future. It advises rethinking the relationship of traditional discipline-related and cognitive skills to broadly transferable work-readiness skills. A good summary of options for improving the high school to work transition is given by Brand (1993).

But it is difficult to make significant changes in curriculum as long as career counselors and advisers, vocational faculty, and those responsible for cooperative education programs in the middle and high schools have an outdated view of the workforce. They cannot serve their students well if they still think of manufacturing in Taylorist terms of an assembly line with each worker contributing only a limited task. Counselors are typically overloaded. College-bound students get priority, so others get very little career counseling. What little they get is frequently based on an obsolete picture of career possibilities. When one of the authors of this volume complained that a counselor had advised a neighbor's child to take a lucrative but dead-end job delivering pizza over a more demanding entry-level position in a high-tech company where she might have a future, the assistant superintendent admitted, *"Our counselors know more about getting into the right colleges than about getting into the right job."*

Cooperative education programs are a bright, but tiny, light in the darkness. A well-designed "co-op ed" program combines work-readiness training and introductory learning in a specific career area. It then places students in part-time jobs that add an experiential component to the vocational studies. The students are closely supervised and the outcomes evaluated. Some of the better transition programs are cosponsored by business and industry (e.g., the TRAC/USA program described briefly in Chapter 4 and below). They enjoy the advantage of a combined, deliberate effort to make the work experience meaningful and to integrate its agenda of learning with academic studies.

At most schools that offer cooperative education, however, meaningful integration with academic programs does not occur. Cooperative education means simply that juniors and seniors either find work on their own or are placed in jobs where they work after school. The jobs are chosen without consideration of the skills and competencies involved and with little supervision or on- or off-the-job training. The work experience may mean endless hours refolding and shelving shirts in a clothing store or running the copier in an office or cleaning test tubes in a laboratory. The learning is minimal, the tedium maximal, and the linkage with academic studies nonexistent. Frequently, what students learn is that work is difficult, unrewarding, and poorly paid. The result is a young person who enters the workforce with negative attitudes and expectations. Clearly, there are better ways to manage the school-to-work transition.

The TRAC/USA™ program of Dusco Community Services is an example. This program recruits high-school juniors and seniors at risk of not making a successful transition from school to work. In effect, it shepherds them through that transition, providing support and mentoring. TRAC/USA does not treat training, development of a good work ethic, and the acquisition of basic intellectual and work skills as three separate affairs. It integrates them into a single endeavor. The payoff, in current earnings and over the longer term for a career with multiple possibilities, is apparent to students and helps to motivate them.

Such programs should be in operation throughout the United States. Existing school services should be transformed to achieve this integration of counseling, career planning, educational planning, mentoring on work ethic and skills, and transition management for all students, not just for the disadvantaged and those at highest risk. Whether Dusco can become self-supporting without philanthropic or public support of its labor-intensive youth-development elements is not clear. But it is clear that, like Head Start for young children, this form of Head Start for youth would be a good social investment.

In *The Neglected Majority* (1985), Dale Parnell, former president of the American Association of Community and Junior Colleges, refers to students of all ages who need more than a high-school education but less than four years of college to qualify as workers and citizens in today's world. He, too, pleads for an orchestration of the transition from lower schools into post-secondary education and from there into work. In essence, Parnell points out that current curricular patterns, coupled with the looseness of institutional guidance arrangements and the inability of families to help youth negotiate the transition from school to work, mean a great waste of youth time and public resources on studies that add up to neither a meaningful college sequel nor a viable transition into jobs.

FROM COLLEGE TO WORK

The transition from colleges and universities to jobs is only slightly better managed than that from high school to work. Colleges involve themselves actively in placing their graduating students, but the level of career counseling is usually not much more sophisticated than that of the high schools. For students who have not pursued an academic path that is clearly career related, where to begin the job search can be a bewildering question.

As of 1987, 60 percent of college students were 23 or older (NCES 1990). An increasing proportion of students of traditional age have "stopped out" between high school and college, taking the time for travel, for a break, or for a temporary job before resuming studies. While many college students go on to graduate school before entering full-time work, the most typical route is from college directly to work. (This is also true for students who temporarily stop out or permanently drop out before completing the bachelor's degree.)

The new majority of older adults, who have usually already had five or more years of work experience, are less in need of immediate job placement services when they leave school than of assistance in long-term career planning and/or skills transfer. Career planning services are rarely provided with the sophistication experienced workers require.

Career planning is often further complicated by the problem of skills transfer. Do newly acquired skills, competencies, knowledge, and attitudes transfer back to the workplace? Does the child care worker apply the principles derived from the child psychology course to her work with 12 screaming infants? Is the automotive technician with a new certificate in CAD-CAM design given an opportunity to use her knowledge to design a new engine part? Is the recent MBA encouraged to apply his learning by being assigned new management responsibilities?

Research (e.g., Baldwin and Ford 1988) indicates that this transfer of training usually does *not* occur. Students who have learned valuable skills and problem-solving strategies are typically confronted by work settings that do not support their use. Without this support, the transfer does not occur.

FROM WORK BACK TO SCHOOL

We have discussed the difficulties workers may confront in their return to the classroom: making multiple choices of what to study, where, when, and how. The opportunity to go back to learning is not a benefit unless the nature of the transition is understood and help is proffered to the student-worker who must manage it. Research (e.g., Fisher, Goff, Nadler and Chinsky 1989) shows that individuals typically seek five types of support:

(1) tangible resources such as time, money, materials, transportation, and child care; (2) technical assistance to help get the job done, such as tutors, lab partners, and study groups; (3) advice from experts such as faculty, counselors, or other staff as to what to study or what to do about other matters; (4) emotional support from friends, spouses, or supervisors to help through tough times; and (5) social support in a group of people who either are going through the experience themselves or have gone through it.

In the EGDPs described earlier, these five types of support are available. Help for workers who return to school sometimes takes the form of support from an understanding supervisor, a formal workshop that addresses transition issues, career and education counseling, or simply some advice from a friend who has already accomplished the transition.

Some workplaces actually work against a smooth transition because their culture views those who aspire to higher education as "uppity," or "thinking they're better than us." The National Development and Training Center of UAW/Ford was able to change such a culture, with CAEL's assistance, through an active campaign engaging life and education advisors and using videotapes featuring employees who had made good use of the tuition assistance program. So we stress again: this kind of assistance in the work-to-school transition is an essential part of the successful EGDP.

The success of the EGDPs of UAW/Ford, the Baby Bells, and others previously described (relative to others with similar purpose but lower rates of participation and completion) is due in part to their tight integration of educational planning with career planning, of advising with mentoring and instructional services, of expediting and support services with career and educational processes, and of moral support from both employer and union and personal support of families.

FROM WELFARE TO SCHOOL & WORK

Almost universally perceived as the the most difficult of the transitions to navigate is that from welfare to school and on to work or from welfare directly to work. Almost all programs with this purpose have been heavily subsidized by government and success rates have been relatively low, even when they "skim the cream off the top" (that is, recruit only the most promising candidates). Not so with an enterprise called America Works, a program that is "taking the poor up the hill from public assistance to the labor force." Charlayne Hunter-Gault told the story on the MacNeil-Lehrer NewsHour, 13 June 1990:

America Works is a private profit-making company with branches in New York and Connecticut. During its almost five years of operation, America Works has helped almost 1,000 welfare recipients find jobs — jobs that 90 percent of them still hold.

Orientation is the first stop. The clients find out about America Works mostly through classified ads. .... Next comes ... a pre-employment class, a mandatory, week-long session, where applicants familiarize themselves with routines and work habits like being on time. Also intangibles that help build self-esteem lost through years of debilitating welfare dependency.

[After work on skills] America Works has placed people in entry-level positions in accounting firms, printing, public, fashion, and law offices. One of its unique features is the support that it provides to the worker during a four-month probationary period ... [during which] a company representative visits the site a few days a week to head off any real or potential problems between the worker and the company. It is called "try before you buy." It is also during this time that America Works pays the worker a $3.80

hourly start-up salary. The company pays about $7.00 an hour to cover benefits and other costs. If an employee remains in the job for a year the government gives the employer a tax credit.

America Works was created by Lee Bowes, a sociologist, and her husband, Peter Cove. Cove explained on the MacNeill-Lehrer News Hour that, just as Federal Express privatized what the government was not doing very well with parts of the postal system, America Works is trying to do the same by getting welfare recipients into jobs — at a profit. Many of its clients are dropouts; those who have graduated from high school have limited English and math skills and have had negative experiences with school. The key problems to address with these clients are described as "inappropriate attitudes and behavior." The average client of America Works, at the time of the MacNeill-Lehrer report, had been on welfare for 10 years at an annual welfare cost of $14,000. It cost the government a one-time outlay of $5,000 to get a person off welfare through the America Works program.

WORK AS SCHOOL

In Chapter 4 we told the story of a corporation that at times uses its worksite as a learning site, combining learning and production, thus making the worksite a "school." Though the least deliberately managed of the arenas for workforce learning, day-to-day workplaces are where the greatest part of the learning effort is currently made. As we explain in Chapter 12, they offer the greatest potential for further enhancing worker qualifications. Precisely because of the previous neglect and because of its potency as a site of experience-based learning, the workplace is where the greatest potential learning gain for the outlay of dollars and effort can probably be made in the next decade.

This section has discussed five effective ways to close the skills gap: smoothing the transitions from high school or college to work, from work to school, and from welfare to work, as well as turning the workplace into a school. What should affect the choice in particular cases? And how can workers' qualifications, once achieved, be documented and made known to employers seeking workers?

THE CHOICE OF LEARNING ARENAS

Some of the considerations that will affect the choice of learning arenas for optimizing worker qualifications leap to mind: relative costs, relative convenience of access, attractiveness to the learners, and ability of the providers and the facilities at those sites to supply what is needed. Let us also keep in mind who the learners will be, what else will be going on in their lives, and what they will need to learn.

A recent study of baccalaureate curricula for adults (Keeton 1991) identified seven characteristics that distinguish most groups of adult learners from traditional high school and college students:

1. The greater amount and larger significance of experiences from which they have learned and on which they can draw in their further learning;

2. The greater time pressures under which they labor with their numerous responsibilities (work, family, community);

3. The wider scope and significance of responsibilities recently or currently exercised in their work, family, or volunteer roles;

4. The greater clarity of their reasons for returning to formal studies and the degree of determination with which they are pursuing these purposes;

5. The higher level of intellectual and emotional maturity or development they bring to learning tasks;

6. The more practical nature of their concerns (that is, the extent to which they see the proposed learning as having an early and significant usefulness to them); and

7. More uncertainty about their own ability as learners, given recent absence from formal studies, rusty academic skills, or relative lack of such skills.

This picture of adult learners suggests that the climate of the local high school or residential college for young students is not likely to be congenial to the learning needs of worker-learners. In the traditional high school or college program, an adult's prior experience is typically not valued, the time pressures on older students are not usually considered when assignments are made, and the practical concerns of adult students are not included in course syllabi. For these reasons, a different set of learning arenas is required. The best settings for learning are logistically feasible for adult learners, provide coaching or instruction that fits their learning styles and preferences, and offer support structures and processes that help them cope with time pressures, competing responsibilities, and personal expectations.

CLOSING THE SKILLS GAP: SCALE OF EFFORT & FOCUS OF EFFORT

SCALE OF EFFORT

We estimate (and the estimate may well be substantially too low) that the investment of worker time required to close the skills gap is between two and three times the amount currently devoted to such learning. This estimate is derived from the use of three different approaches: (1) comparing the American training outlay with those of Japan and Germany, (2) comparing the average use of tuition-aid programs among the Fortune 500 with that achieved in the CAEL EGDPs, and (3) analyzing the degree of skills upgrading required by the U.S. workforce and the capacity of the available arenas to provide that upgrading.

Worker-learners are probably already spending all of their time on activities they value. So allocating, say, an average of fifteen hours a week for learning instead of five will mean taking the ten hours away from other activities: time with a spouse or significant other, time with children, time at recreation, or time in church or civic activities. If employers permit some of this added time to be taken during work hours, workers will meet this demand much more readily.

Some directors of corporate training estimate that 90 percent or more of current formal training under corporate auspices never transfers to job sites in terms of improved work practices (Georgenson 1982). If that is true, then corporations that substitute the more fruitful models of training and education discussed here will not need as much add-on time of workers. We believe the targeted learning outcomes of collegiate education could be accomplished by more efficient learning strategies with 35 percent less of the learners' time than is currently used. If, as argued in Chapter 12, the most productive form of learning for workplace uses occurs in work settings designed as learning environments, closing the skills gap may not involve added classroom-based activities. Rather, it may require a redesign of academic studies (with more attention to basic elements of intelligent functioning), worksite learning and work relationships, and the interplay among school and work activities. Such integration of efforts could shorten the path to universal employability and reduce the needed investment of worker time for closing the gap from triple present levels to as little as double those levels.

FOCUS OF EFFORT

The most promising approach for effecting the needed skills development conveniently, inexpensively, and with the best hope of enlisting energetic worker participation is a coalition of employers ready to transform their worksites to learning sites, with brokers similar to the CAEL joint venture teams and with training designers competent to assist with problem identification and training plans. A pool of funds will probably be needed to encourage setting up the coalitions and providing incentives to employers, unions, and workers to give priority to this effort and to appropriate EGDP funds from their employee benefit programs. Such a pool of funds might come initially from state governments, the federal government, and (for venturesome innovative efforts) a small set of very large public foundations.

On the basis of CAEL's experience in its EGDPs, we strongly believe that the recommended effort cannot achieve optimal results without following certain key principles, discovered through the pioneering ventures already reported. These principles (see Chapters 11 and 12) are of course not set in stone; they will probably evolve and be improved through continued scrutiny. As a starting point, however, they seem to us essential.

CREDENTIALING

At present, the learning system in this country is rich and varied. People learn throughout their lives, in formal educational institutions, in schools and colleges, and in structured programs in companies, unions, the armed services, government, churches, and community organizations. People also learn informally through work, recreation, hobbies, travel, reading, and various electronic media, and by talking to and observing family, friends, neighbors, and mentors. In short, they learn through both doing and experiencing in many arenas of life.

PROBLEMS WITH THE CURRENT SYSTEM

As powerful as this learning system is, however, it is also painfully fragmented and rife with redundancies, particularly as far as vocational learning is concerned. Colleges recognize high school diplomas, though they complain a lot about the quality of high school graduates and have developed stringent criteria for selecting some, rejecting others.

Far more complicated, however, are the problems of transferring that the student faces when trying to cope with the varying standards for credit within and among colleges and universities. Will a course or even a degree from College A be accepted by College B? Will the level of writing skill that enabled Michael to pass freshman English 101 at College A guarantee his having the background skills to pass freshman English 102 when he changes schools? What about Janine, an older student who has earned 20 credits at the community college through prior learning assessment of her work-based knowledge of sales and marketing? Will the baccalaureate program in business to which she is applying accept those 20 credits?

These are problems with which traditional college-age students have been grappling for years. But they intensify when adults are involved in the system, especially when they bring with them important learning that was acquired outside the traditional classroom. Universities recognize associate and baccalaureate degrees, though they will not always accept them in toto when a student transfers, nor will they open their graduate programs to all who have completed an undergraduate degree. Not all credits nor all degrees are treated as equal.

Although many colleges and universities have begun to take seriously the learning that people acquire on their own or through sponsored courses and will assess that learning for college credit, not all institutions accept in transfer the credit for prior learning assessed by another institution. And although the American Council on Education, through its PONSI and other assessment programs, recommends credits for those industry, union, government, and military training programs that it has evaluated, not all colleges accept these recommendations. Recognition of nontraditionally acquired learning is still a crazy-quilt affair, lacking a common national goal and a common currency (current practices are summarized in Fugate and Chapman 1992).

TOWARD A NATIONAL CREDENTIALING SYSTEM

The only commonly agreed-upon currencies of learning in the United States are credits, diplomas, degrees, and certificates. The educational establishment has a monopoly on three out of four of these. (The standards for certificates are looser than are the other three and more loosely controlled. They may be issued for everything from a 10-course college program in managing information systems to a four-hour, company-sponsored workshop in stress reduction.)

Credit, the coinage in colleges and universities, is particularly well entrenched. The concept is reinforced by transfer agreements among institutions, state funding formulas for institutions, and a general perception that the credit represents something "real," solid, a measure of learning, competence, or mastery. One college credit (semester-hour credit) is generally agreed to represent about 15 or 16 hours of classroom time plus roughly two hours of study by the student for each formal hour of instruction.

The use of the credit as the measure of learning gets more complicated when colleges, in their prior learning assessment programs for adults, attempt to equate noncourse-derived learning with college-level learning. The criterion of time spent is inadequate to measure learning. The concepts of "college level," "depth," "breadth," and "theoretical versus practical" further complicate the translation into academic terms. It is to their credit that so many colleges, in the interests of their adult students, are building reputations for fair, valid, and reliable assessment programs. But for all the esteem in which it is held, academic credit rests upon no universally accepted criteria in learning terms. Its weight varies from institution to institution and has no measurable relationship to specific units of learning or to competencies.

What does all of this mean for working adults who have gained significant knowledge, skills, or competencies on the job but for whom these are not recognized if they lack some form of validation? Do the adults all have to register for college courses, whether or not they want further formal education in order to have their learning assessed? What does it mean for the U.S. economy, which depends on a skilled workforce but has no reliable means of locating people with the specific skills needed for a specific job? What does it mean for the personnel director hiring for skilled jobs, who must largely take on faith that time spent on task equals learning, though common sense and reality would dictate otherwise?

Imagine a national system of credentialing that embraced formal education as well as company-, government-, and union-sponsored learning, informal on-the-job training, and individuals' self-education through all the means that this learning system provides. Imagine that this nation was motivated enough and wise enough to involve industry groups and unions in devising sets of competencies that would represent the various levels of mastery of a broad range of vocational skills, from chicken inspection to retail sales to hydraulic engineering to financial management. Suppose further that tests of skills demonstrations could be agreed on that would accurately measure people's degrees of competence in all of these fields. Finally, suppose that for each person these data were summarized in a profile of competence and knowledgeability and recorded in a national databank available to employers looking for workers, companies seeking to relocate, and economists making labor projections.

We propose here a national system of credentialing that focuses on the profile of qualifications rather than on the source through which it was acquired. If this idea sounds high-flown, think again. Already in place are some highly successful apprenticeship training programs, concrete examples of how this system can work. Also, a credentialing system suitable for the United States was described in a paper delivered at the National Governors' Association's 1989 conference, *Toward a Credentialing System for Postsecondary Education and Its Partners* (Spille 1989). Its author, Henry A. Spille, is vice president and director of the Center for Adult Learning and Educational Credentials of the American

Council on Education. Furthermore, the proposal has sparked serious discussion among the business community, union leaders, educators, and government officials. The government of Australia is considering a somewhat similar idea for a "Skills Bank" (Docking 1990).

The important concept in both the U.S. and Australian models is that once a benchmark for competence has been established, *skills demonstrated are considered of equal merit for recording or crediting, irrespective of the source of the learning.* (This assumes that the assessor is licensed to assess such skills by some official body that will manage this enterprise.)

A major boost to the drive for job skills standards occurred when the U.S. Departments of Labor and Education initiated public dialogue on voluntary, industry-based skill standards and certification in March 1992. The two departments announced in late October 1992 a set of grants to national trade associations and education groups to develop job skill standards for their respective industries, and published in December 1992 an analysis of findings of the earlier public dialogue. Ninety-one percent of responses in that dialogue had been favorable to such a development, with most opposition coming from fears that the idea poses a threat to the existing national registered apprenticeship system and related collective bargaining and that some already disenfranchised workers might be further disadvantaged (see Chapter 10). By March 1993, 13 pilot projects were underway in industry groups such as retail sales, metalworking, health technology, electronics, tourism, and automotive technology. A set of principles derived from the public dialogue had been articulated as a guide for the skills standards development (Office of Work-Based Learning 1992).

BENEFITS OF SKILLS CREDENTIALING

The benefits of such a credentialing or skills bank system would extend to all of the partners in the learning enterprise (Docking

1990). Employees would gain an up-to-date cumulative record of skills achieved; a transportable skills transcript that could be used in other regions or in other occupational classifications; and recognition of skills acquired in any situation, including school, the workplace, and their own other experience. They would also gain ready identification of skills deficiencies for which they could seek appropriate training; skills-based information to assist in career and education planning; self-esteem from having a tangible record of achievement; and empowerment to take greater responsibility for their own futures.

Employers would gain verification of employee skills; up-to-date in-house skills audits to identify hidden assets or skills shortfalls; increased flexibility in utilizing these skills across a broader spectrum of jobs; and skills-based recruitment and selection services using regional databases. They would also gain access to skills resource data for planning, performance management, training, promotion, and dismissal; and better information on which to base short- and long-term personnel decisions.

Industries would gain the definition of skills to match current needs of their respective industries; improvement of workforce skills in both range and level for new and current employees; skills resource data to identify potential locations for new industries; and rapid response to the skill demands of new occupational categories.

Unions would gain protection of occupational status in times of structural change; definition and maintenance of occupational entry requirements; and equal opportunity for equal skills. They would also gain assistance in linking salary levels to skill levels and a better way to link worker training with career development.

Educators and human resource managers would gain validation and accreditation of curriculum and assessment methods on a skills basis; learning requirements stated in terms of output skills; and regional skills audits to assist in predicting learning demands. They would also gain curriculum effectiveness validated on a skills-delivered basis and responsibility for providing the learning for which they are the most appropriate resource, whether they represent colleges, vocational schools, on-the-job learning sites, or in-house, formal, or informal training.

National, state, and local governments would gain more accurate targeting of regional and group needs; reduced demand for emergency labor market programs; improved forecasting and planning data; and improved national productivity in the economy.

All partners would gain a common framework, database, and language for making decisions in matters relating to industry relocation, employment, career ladders, salaries, human resource management, and education and training. Unfortunately, many practical, financial, and territorial hurdles must be overcome before such an outcome can be achieved. But this was also the case for prior learning assessment twenty years ago, and that program is now widely accepted and supported by both business and educators.

A national credentialing system of the kind here proposed would greatly reduce the difficulties we have described in the transitions among welfare, school, and work.

SEARCHING FOR A JOB

This chapter is about transitions, but it has centered on transitions in the development of skills integral to the jobs to be performed. Employability, however, requires also the ability to land a job when one is unemployed or when one has resigned from, or been laid off from, a previous job. The recent recession has made clear that not even white-collar workers are immune to layoff.

There is a long history of programs of training specifically to get jobs and to advance within a work career. Research on this topic shows remarkable results in that individuals who receive training in job search and strategies are more likely to get a new job than their untrained counterparts (Veth 1993). Severance arrangements in many corporations include assistance with job search. Some skill-development programs, such as America Works, also build placement into their service design. Apprenticeship and cooperative education programs give participants the advantage of being tried out in the work they seek, and often later employed as regular employees by the same employers. Some EGDPs have included opportunities to acquire job search skills, career guidance services, and help with understanding the emerging changes in the pattern of job opportunities. Federal and state programs on youth unemployment have sought to assure placement of their trainees, while some welfare programs provide help in getting off of welfare into work. Research on job search strategies and services nevertheless pinpoints a major need to increase the job-seeking strategies of unemployed workers (Veth 1993). In a sense, job-seeking skills themselves are essential for employability.

10

AVOIDING A TWO-TIERED SOCIETY

Will an effective drive toward increasing the proportion of productively employable workers in the United States actually
worsen the situation of those who are already at a disadvantage?
The danger of creating a two-tiered society is real, in part because
disadvantages such as illiteracy among those currently unemployed or in low-level jobs limit their access to the further training,
education, and work opportunities that could let them qualify for
better-paying or more secure jobs.

If this gap in starting advantages between segments of the
population persists, it will cause the employability gap to widen.
The differences in time out of work, the pay levels, and opportunities for advancement and employment security will widen.
Historically, the terms "haves" and "have-nots" have referred to
income and wealth. But they may increasingly be seen as more a
matter of education and training, the essential preconditions of
keeping a job and advancing in a career. How can the starting
disadvantages of those who are currently underqualified be overcome or prevented?

CATCH-22: THE COMPOUNDING
CIRCLE OF DISADVANTAGE

There are different kinds of starting disadvantages in employability. All of them compound themselves, since they not only

diminish a worker's value to an employer in the immediate job but also hinder him or her from becoming qualified for better-paying and more responsible work. Hong Tan's 1988 survey of private-sector training in the United States reveals different levels of training opportunities that contribute to a widening gap between haves and have nots. He identifies five areas where the discrepancies in training opportunities are especially great: race, gender, previous education, native language, and years of work experience.

RACE

Tan provides sobering perspectives on training differences by race. During their first 13 years of employment, 38.8 percent of white employees receive training. In contrast, only 27.2 percent of nonwhite employees have the benefit of training during this same period. Racial differences were most marked for more advanced training: 19 percent of whites received managerial training compared with only 8 percent of nonwhites, and 44 percent of whites received professional and technical training versus 24 percent of nonwhites. Other studies yield comparable findings on the role of race as a factor in limiting training opportunities.

GENDER

The perspectives on gender are also striking. In all occupations except transportation, women are less likely to receive company training than men. This discrepancy holds for both getting jobs and upgrading skills, although training differences by sex are more pronounced for getting jobs. When women are systematically deprived of training, they are locked into job categories that form a glass ceiling on salaries and promotions.

PREVIOUS EDUCATION & TRAINING

Statistics show that prior education is an essential precondition for professional training and development. Lack of education and training is the single most distinguishing characteristic of the poor. Among economically disadvantaged people, only 10.9 percent of men and 12 percent of women report receiving any postsecondary training relevant to their work. Lacking preparation for the workplace, they are unlikely to be trained: only 2.6 percent of disadvantaged men and 2.3 percent of disadvantaged women report receiving training from their employers. Less than 1 percent of corporate training budgets is devoted to what Xerox chairman David Kearns calls "product recall work for the public school system."

The picture is very different for educated employees. Employers train only 45 percent of their employees who failed to complete high school, but they train 71 percent of those who did and 79 percent of college graduates. Employees who are trained in one job are also more likely than other employees to be trained in subsequent jobs.

These differences are further accentuated for professional and technical training: only 7 percent of employees who did not graduate from high school received this type of training, compared with 27 percent of high-school graduates, 44 percent of those with some postsecondary education, and 56 percent of employees who were college graduates.

Tan's findings are confirmed by a study by the Commission on the Skills of the American Workforce (1990). That study found that two thirds of company training dollars go to the college educated. The breakdown is 27 percent to professionals, 22 percent to managers, 9 percent to sales professionals, and 8 percent to technicians and supervisors. Only 34 percent of training dollars go to clerical, retail sales, and service workers, laborers, and technicians (49). In its study of productivity in America, an MIT commission concluded:

"There seems to be a systematic underevaluation in this country of how much difference it can make when people are well educated and when their skills are continuously developed and challenged. This

> *underestimation of human resources becomes a self-fulfilling prophecy for it translates into a pattern of training for work that turns out badly educated workers with skills that are narrow and hence vulnerable to rapid obsolescence."* (Dertouzos, Lester, and Solow 1989, 82).

This pattern not only accentuates the problems of those with initial disadvantages but also works against the best interests of employers as they seek to increase competitiveness and profitability. While the United States focuses its training efforts on management, foreign governments have massive programs to help companies give ongoing training to hourly employees in the skills of the 1990s (Magaziner and Patimkin 1989, x). Employer training, therefore, accentuates differences in educational attainment and achievement among employees — differences that account for most of the differences in income among workers.

NATIVE LANGUAGE

Those for whom English is a second language, especially those who migrate to the United States without a beginning knowledge of American English in its spoken and written forms, are at an even further disadvantage in the competition to qualify for jobs with potential of ongoing employment security and rising income. When training opportunities arise, these individuals are not selected to participate. The net result is a widening of the skills gap.

YEARS OF WORK EXPERIENCE

Among those on a similar footing as to race, gender, and previous education and training, employees with more than five years of work experience but more than ten working years before retirement are most likely to receive further training from their employers.

THE SCOPE OF THE PROBLEM OF DISADVANTAGED WORKERS

Clearly, the presence of starting disadvantages in the workplace is a serious problem. We need to ask how widespread it is. How many potential workers are involved? How substantial is their handicap? Consider some highlights about the nature of the U.S. workforce as late as 1989 and projections for the year 2000, according to the Office of Technological Assessment (1990).

■ More than 22 percent of the workforce in the year 2000 will be immigrants.

■ Of that workforce, more than one fifth will be black (11.7 percent) or Hispanic (10.1 percent).

■ While a record high proportion (67 percent) of all Americans over the age of 16 were working in 1989, this is mainly because twice as many women were working in 1989 as in 1969. Two thirds of the employment growth in the mid-1990s is expected to be among women.

■ By the year 2000, at least 15 percent of the workforce will need annual retraining because of mobility.

■ In the year 2000, 12.3 percent of the workforce will be at least 55 years old.

■ As of 1988, 34.8 percent of blacks and 27.4 percent of Hispanics in the United States had at least one year of college.

From another source (OERI's National Center for Educational Statistics), we learn that participation rates in postsecondary education are higher for blacks and Hispanics 25 to 34 years old than for whites. The opposite is true for 18- to 24-year-olds. The data suggest that the older minority student is usually not a re-entry student but a first-time adult college student (1988). Such a student will be unfamiliar with the basic language, procedures, expectations, and culture of college and will need in-depth support and orientation services to succeed. A subsequent OERI study (1990) confirms these trends.

An important implication of these studies is that starting disadvantages among the American workers are on a scale that can substantially lower the competitiveness of enterprises staffed by them. *"In the competitive arena, the issue is not what disadvantaged workers* will *do when motivated but rather what they* can *do, given their weaker basic education, the level of work experiences provided by companies with low regard for training, and the few companies with institutional resources that enable them to train such workers"* (Dertouzos, Lester, and Solow 1989, 22).

This catalog of starting disadvantages and forms of their compounding makes it clear that "business as usual" will yield a widening gap in employment, income, and career advancement. To allow that gap to persist and grow is to invite polarization within our society and to raise the ensuing social costs (discussed in Chapter 7) that drain state economies.

OVERCOMING THE PATTERN OF DISADVANTAGE

In January 1990, the Quality Education for Minorities Project, based at the Massachusetts Institute of Technology, published a report that further documents the problems just described and proposes measurable goals, implementation strategies, and policy recommendations aimed at overcoming them. Among the goals, for example, is to triple (to 264,000) the number of minority baccalaureates from the 1987 number. Another is to quadruple (to 68,000) the number of minority baccalaureates in the physical and life sciences and engineering by the year 2000. Other telling recommendations follow:

■ Revise federal financial aid formulas to increase the proportion of grants to loans.

■ Offer six-week summer science residential programs for at least 50 minority high-school juniors on each college and university campus.

■ Increase outreach efforts at the precollege level. (We would add an outreach effort within the currently disadvantaged workforce.)

■ Improve the racial climate of schools and colleges.

■ Link salary and promotion decisions on teachers to effectiveness in facilitating the graduation of minority students.

■ Modify institutional accreditation criteria to include assessment of institutional climate for minority students.

■ Make college and career options known to children beginning in middle school. (Again, we would add comparable efforts for those already in the workforce or out of school and unemployed.)

■ Increase the number and quality of counselors, including bilingual counselors. (A similar need exists among already employed but disadvantaged workers.)

A number of means are available to close the gap in starting advantages and arrest its tendency to widen. They include (1) changes in the focus of schooling in public elementary and secondary education and vocational-technical training institutions; (2) refocusing and reallocation of employers' training activities; (3) increased private-sector enterprises for integrated recruiting, training, apprenticeship, and placement services for at-risk and unemployed youth and elderly; and (4) incentives from federal and state governments for public and private-sector providers of training. These would include literacy training, development of basic work skills, and advanced education and training to offset the starting disadvantages.

PUBLIC SCHOOLING

Chapter 9 discussed refocusing the approach to the transition from school to work and identified provisions that would prevent starting disadvantages in the workplace for some people leaving school. How should we refocus? Toward a client-centered orientation. The supposed child-centeredness of schools is pursued within a more fundamental commitment to certain curricula and institutional imperatives that belie a primary focus on what the client — whether child or returning worker — needs. Particularly for adults who are concurrently working and studying or for young adults about to enter the workforce, we need a relentless focus on what the student needs to succeed and advance in the workplace. This focus need not diminish attention to citizenship duties or self-development. But career development and success should have equal priority with these other concerns.

EMPLOYER-SPONSORED TRAINING

Chapters 11 and 12 will discuss how employers can help to remove starting handicaps. Two major types of refocusing, relative to disadvantaged employees, are needed. First, the disproportionate investment in better-educated, higher-level employees must be corrected. We do not argue for spending the same amount on each employee, but we do contend that every employee needs further education and training and should have the same opportunity to get what is most appropriate for him or her. Second, reorienting training to business problems (see Chapter 12) and making all levels of workers part of teams that cut across hierarchic levels are especially important for disadvantaged workers.

PRIVATE-SECTOR INITIATIVES

In the summer of 1990 (as reported in Chapter 9), public attention was drawn to an innovative attack upon chronic unemployment and welfare status by a profit-making enterprise called America

Works, which recruited, trained, and counseled welfare recipients and then placed them in paid jobs. This enterprise selected welfare clients for their desire to escape from welfare; assessed their work skills (including reading, speaking, and mathematics); provided the training essential to initial work placements; and obtained those placements under contracts with employers. The brokering enterprise continued to monitor and coach trainees in becoming reliable, productive employees. In effect, the enterprise made money carrying out a function that public agencies do less well at taxpayer expense.

Also in 1990 Dusco Community Services, with the assistance of CAEL, began developing the previously mentioned TRAC/USA™ program. This program selects and recruits at-risk high-school students. It trains them for employment in retail businesses, places each in a series of four apprenticeships in retailing, helps them plan a career in that field with promise of advancement (an opportunity not normally offered by entry-level jobs in small businesses), and continues as their employer of last resort (as a provider of temporary service workers).

These models demonstrate the feasibility of enabling substantial proportions of unemployed people to get themselves on the path toward self-support and advancement, thus overcoming the starting disadvantages that frustrate so many others. Bringing such activity to a scale commensurate with the need in the United States today, however, calls for a massive increase in such services.

GOVERNMENT INCENTIVES

The examples we have provided of successful efforts to help people out of dependency and unemployability are often a financial gamble for their leaders. They are generally done on a small scale because of the upfront costs and risks involved. Government incentives could increase the number of such efforts without diminishing their enterprising nature. In Chapter 7 we identified some basic incentives available to government. For example, treating employer-provided education benefits as nontaxable to the recipient would be more important to entry-level or disadvantaged workers than to higher-paid, more secure managerial employees. Another suggestion is to prohibit the lowering of welfare benefits when a person's use of education benefits is an essential incentive.

COPING WITH MULTIPLE BARRIERS

A common problem of efforts to overcome disadvantage is that a hundred factors interact to create the problem, while the attack on it is generally uncoordinated and limited to a few of those factors. The successful innovations discussed earlier in this book exemplify ways of using partnerships to mount a cohesive, integrated attack on such multifaceted problems. How can this idea be harnessed to help disadvantaged entry-level workers?

Essential to an assisting agency's responsiveness to a disadvantaged person's need is grasping the problem whole, being able almost intuitively to discern how specific interventions will either precipitate new problems or work successfully in the face of countervailing forces. One tool in getting such insight is to remember that the working adult has to to function simultaneously in at least three to five major roles, which compete with one another for his or her time, resources, and emotional and mental energies. The typical working adult is also a spouse and parent and may play a significant role in a parent-teacher organization, church, or other community endeavor. In addition, for many people leisure activity is critical to mental and physical health. If a worker needs further education and training to remove his or her disadvantage and to stay qualified for work and for advancement, how can this added activity be managed in combination with the other roles?

It is useless for the supervisor or educational adviser to tell the worker what to do about needed education or training if its impact on his or her other roles and duties is not acknowledged and resolved. We believe that the remarkable participation and success rates of the CAEL-corporate-union employability programs are due in part to their provisions for counseling and support services based on a grasp of the adult worker-learner's total situation. Moreover, if a support person grasps this concept, so may the worker-learner. That insight can be a powerful aid to more effective self-management.

A second aid to coping with multiple barriers is the practice of relevant profiling. Consider the contrast between (a) an adult who is a Chinese-American, the child of a family that owns a small business, and the first generation of her family to attend school in the United States and (b) an adult who is a Vietnamese refugee without supporting spouse or family, in her late twenties with a dependent child, trying to work her way onto and up a career ladder appropriate to her abilities. One can readily imagine a score of pictures, filled in with critical details affecting the ability to combine work with further education and training. Each picture will indicate to a work supervisor, college teacher, or counselor a different form of intervention. Relevant profiling means developing an array of such pictures so that those who interact with these worker-learners can find the best ways to help them to remove their starting disadvantages.

AN ATTITUDE TOWARD DISADVANTAGE

There is a view within the human services field today that efforts to help disadvantaged persons have often compounded the problems addressed because of a fundamental underlying attitude that fosters dependency. By viewing "disadvantaged persons" as different from individuals who are in a position to "help," we foster their segregation into groups of like persons. We treat them as unable to contribute to meeting others' needs and wants, and we entrench patterns of self-doubt and dependency.

What if we took the attitude instead that everyone has some kind of disadvantage and everyone has the capacity to help someone else with problems? Nothing can be more important to removing disadvantage than building self-respect and self-esteem. Having people assume some responsibility, however small, for helping others overcome their distinctive obstacles could have a transforming effect. It would generate a climate of peers collaborating in problem solving rather than one of superiors providing gracious services to the needy.

4

PULLING IT ALL TOGETHER

Are there guiding principles and policies that emerge from research and from experience with employability programs to date?

PART 4

is devoted to answering this question.

In Chapter 11

we draw extensively on the experience of the Council for Adult and Experiential Learning to extract lessons learned from more than a score of employee growth and development programs. Related research is used to throw light on those experiences. Ten principles are articulated as the outcome of this analysis.

In Chapter 12

a parallel effort is made to identify principles that can help employers achieve worksites that combine productivity with ongoing workforce development.

Chapter 13

reviews the key findings and recommendations of the preceding chapters of the book and discusses four needs that must be met for an effective nationwide employability effort to be instituted. Those needs are an overall vision and governing policies for that effort, financing, an effective coordination of efforts, and provision of incentives for ongoing energetic cooperation among all of the essential players.

THE PRINCIPLES OF
EFFECTIVE EMPLOYABILITY PROGRAMS

For employees such as John, Jules, and Joan to be productive on an ongoing basis, three essentials must be in place. First, they must have the skills required to do their jobs. Second, they must be motivated to use those skills. Finally, they must work in an environment that supports and encourages the use of their skills (Porter and Lawler 1968). This chapter describes how the employee growth and development concept, employing these principles, can help workers develop and maintain productive skills, moving them toward the goal of enhanced employability.

We integrate here insights from research on adult learning (e.g., Cross 1981; Brookfield 1986) and from CAEL's experiences over the past eight years in designing and managing employability programs for a number of large national and international corporations, unions, and government agencies covering tens of thousands of workers, in many settings and for many purposes. The integration of theory and experience provides a framework of 10 principles that can be used to develop effective EGDPs for a variety of situations and clienteles.

In their totality, the 10 principles that follow provide a dynamic that drives training for employment to optimal success.

PRINCIPLE 1:
GIVE LEARNER-WORKERS CHOICES

Principle 1 is the *sine qua non* of employee growth and development programs: give learner-workers choices. The stumbling block for most training programs is that they subordinate the needs of the trainees to other concerns. Tuition assistance programs, which were created to encourage worker development and enhance worker morale, have usually put the choice of courses taken and educational goals pursued under the employer's control. Tuition payments are usually restricted to courses directly related to the employee's current job or to a prospective job within the company. Where greater latitude is allowed, the employee must usually obtain approval of courses or programs from a supervisor or the manager of the tuition aid program.

These controls were intended to make sure that employers got their money's worth and that better returns for an employee's work would redound to the employer's benefit. The piper called the tune, but sometimes no one danced. Indeed, the national average for participation in employer-sponsored, nonmandated training programs has hovered between 3 and 5 percent (Charner et al. 1978). This history contrasts with rates of 20 to 30 percent or more in course enrollments (not just use of counseling services, career planning workshops, and the like) in a number of CAEL-managed employability programs that gave learner-workers choices.

Even in state or federally sponsored programs, the individual worker has seldom been a key part of the planning or implementation process. Many government-funded employability programs begin by analyzing the job market, current and local needs of industry and business, and near-term economic forecasts for the region. The best of these analyses try to determine how many jobs are likely to open up in which sectors and what skills those jobs will call for. States, cities, and counties are spending thousands of dollars gathering and interpreting workforce data and using the results to establish short-term training programs. But these programs may not address the actual needs of the workplace or individual workers by the time the participants graduate.

Faceless workers, moved about from program to program like pieces on a Monopoly board (we reject the chess metaphor as too deliberate), may or may not succeed in completing their training, finding new jobs, functioning successfully in those jobs, and finding their new skills still in demand five years out. Whether they do or not, they are hostage to forces outside their control. Unfortunately, current attempts to forecast which skills will be needed a few years from now, or even to define the evolving nature of new jobs, are based on inadequate data. We do not know for certain what specific knowledge and skills workers should be acquiring — as distinct from generic skills (named in Chapter 8). Indeed, narrow, job-specific skills are probably the least useful in the long run.

Too many employability programs are not talking with the intended recipients to find out how their interests, skills, and values may determine the kinds of training in which they will succeed; how their attitudes and life situations may be preventing them from taking advantage of training opportunities; and what life and career goals they have or can be encouraged to think about.

The question is not just which courses or programs workers should be taking. *The real question is how to help workers determine what choices are best for their individual situations in a changing job market.* For a learning program to succeed, the learner's motivation and persistence in pursuing it are crucial. To keep motivation and persistence high, the learner must have an active role in deciding what to learn and why; be involved in the choice of provider, scheduling, and other key decisions; and, finally, understand what the other stakeholders have to gain from his or her participation.

WORKER CONTRIBUTIONS
TO EMPLOYABILITY PROGRAMS

The employee invests in the success of the learning enterprise at least as much as the sponsor. An employee engaged in a training program that takes place outside the workplace inevitably incurs both monetary and nonmonetary costs. The monetary costs may include transportation to school, parking fees, incidental educational expenses not paid for by tuition aid (even textbooks are frequently not covered), child care, and, in some cases, the need to give up a second job.

Nonmonetary costs to the worker can be even more significant. Returning to the classroom means spending time away from family and friends, foregoing recreational activities, and structuring one's life in a whole new fashion to fit in class and extra hours for study. It means renegotiating with the family to be relieved of some household duties, adjusting schedules and finding space and privacy for study, and justifying the inconvenience to oneself and to loved ones. These choices require a personal cost-benefit analysis that may force some very difficult decisions.

The employability venture certainly cannot be set up so that the learner alone dictates all conditions and benefits no matter how much it costs other partners or how little they benefit. The effective employability program must pay off for all partners. *But the worker must be treated as one of those partners,* as an active and informed participant.

A PROFILE OF THE NEW LEARNER-WORKERS

Looking at the industrial, service, and technical workers who are the target of most of this new generation of education and training programs (in contrast with more traditional programs focused on management personnel), one finds a predominance of people who have not been well served by the current educational system. There is a high rate of functional illiteracy among what used to be called blue-collar workers.

Even among those who managed to negotiate the system well enough to receive a high-school diploma, education all too often has connotations of oppression, coercion, inefficiency, or even failure. Many working adults regard their 12 years or so in public schools in less than positive terms. Unlike their more highly educated peers, they are not eager to go back for more. Moreover, the family or peer culture rarely offers workers, especially women, either precedent or support for continuing education. The psychological adjustments involved in a return to the classroom in this situation are awesome to contemplate, particularly if the worker's earlier educational experience has left a bad taste.

New student services, modes of delivery, and even curricula and course content developed over the past 10 or 15 years to serve middle-class adult students are frequently inadequate to meet the needs of service and technical workers whose educational background is likely to be less sophisticated and whose demands for support and direct vocational relevance are greater.

It is thus doubly important that worker-learners be made fully aware of their stake in joint ventures for employability. They also need a clear sense of how they can benefit and contribute so that they can become active partners in creating their own employment security. It is only then that they can fully address the choices of what to learn, where to learn it, and why.

PRINCIPLE 2:
PROVIDE LEARNER-WORKERS THE TOOLS THEY NEED TO MAKE INFORMED CHOICES

To be involved in making decisions about their own further education and training, learner-workers must have information about their own needs, aptitudes, skills, and values; current changes in the national and local job markets and in the prospects for continued work with their current employer; and the structures and resources of the various education institutions. They also need a consumer's guide to the educational and training opportunities available.

The Returning to Learning® workshop was originally designed by CAEL for the UAW/Ford College and University Options Program (CUOP). It addresses those real and perceived dispositional and situational barriers that adults face in going back to school and helps them make informed choices about the education and training they will pursue. The workshop pays special attention to building participants' self-confidence, since low self-esteem could inhibit them from full participation in the learning process.

Using highly participative, experiential techniques, the workshop helps the participants explore six topics:

1. *Self-assessment:* those skills, aptitudes, values, and interests they must take into account when making career decisions;

2. *The economic context in which they are functioning:* a reality test of the immediate and projected environment (with emphasis on the job market and hot and cold sectors) and a crash course in how to spot trends, do job research, write a resume, and handle interviews;

3. *Ways to choose the right provider:* how to define their own needs from and demands on the educational institution and how to choose among specific schools in the immediate geographic area to get the right programs and other resources;

4. *How colleges and other schools operate:* their language and culture; the increasing number of adults in the classroom (message: you won't be the only one on campus with graying hair and a mortgage); the difference between the school experience for young people and that for adults; the existing structure of credits, degrees, certificates, and nondegree study; and some nontraditional options;

5. *The concept of adults as nonstop, self-managing learners:* how and what we learn outside the classroom, how this informal or experiential learning helps us in more formal situations and may even be translated into college credit, how to go about having their noncollege-derived learning assessed, and which local colleges have assessment programs; and

6. *Ways adults survive in school:* building a personal support network of family and friends; tips on study skills; time management for the working student; finding and using the school's resources; and the hidden costs of education in time, money, and stress.

This workshop formula has been tailored for different clients in ways that may alter order, time, content, and emphasis, and the ideas and materials have been adapted in response to differing human resource development needs. But the underlying principles remain true to the workshop's original purpose. In all versions, the basic objective is to *empower learners to make informed decisions about their own careers and education.*

By the end of a Returning to Learning workshop, each participant is expected to have completed a preliminary action plan. The plan should include choices of vocational areas to be pursued; long-term goals (e.g., getting a high school equivalency certificate, completing a certificate program in data processing, or getting a job in a major accounting firm); and "next steps," a list of what must be done immediately to begin to put the long-range plan into action.

Clearly a workshop alone, whether eight hours or 50 hours, cannot answer all of the workers' questions, allay all their anxieties, or solve all their problems. In most EGDPs, the workshop is followed up by an optional career and education counseling component that explores further the implications of the self-assessment exercises, sharpens the connections between what has been learned and the individual's own realistic career goals, and assists people in making informed choices about what, where, and when they will study.

PRINCIPLE 3:
ENSURE ADVOCACY BY ALL PARTNERS

The overt and active advocacy of employability programs by every partner is essential if EGDPs are to achieve their maximum effectiveness. The benefits and terms of advocacy should be spelled out early in the process of negotiation between partners. Positive identification with the program should be an ongoing objective of all participants.

All parties to an EGDP must be clear about why they are involved and what they hope to gain. Each partner should understand the others' stake in the program, their respective roles, and the potential points of divisiveness.

The worker who is the immediate beneficiary of the employability program is the all too frequently forgotten partner. He or she must be included in the information network. The initial reaction of employees to any new program always contains an element of distrust. Indeed, some well-meaning programs, introduced without adequate explanation, have foundered on the rock of employee suspicion: "Why do they want me to go to school?" "Are they getting ready to fire me?" "What's the catch?" "Is this a plot to undermine my union?" "Does this mean I'm not doing my job well enough?" These are legitimate questions that must be put to rest so employees can trust the motives behind the "benefit" and function as true partners in the venture.

There are many ways for a hostile or even merely lukewarm partner to sabotage a program. If companies have agreed to the program reluctantly to appease the union, they may not communicate sufficiently about it to workers, refuse to make promised shift-scheduling adjustments, or even discourage participation. If unions are suspicious that the program is the company's way of moving workers into nonunion-covered positions, fear that it will erode worker loyalty, or think it is a means to evade work rules, they have many resources at hand to sabotage the program.

It must be noted, however, that such dire efforts at sabotage are rare. A well-conceived, well-managed employability program quickly gains advocates and creates stronger relationships among the partners on the basis of broader understanding.

PRINCIPLE 4:
PROVIDE ACCESS FOR EVERYONE

The most effective employability program is one that is available to all employees in a given workforce. This includes management and nonmanagement and those who are secure in their jobs or at risk, already sufficiently trained for the jobs they hold or not, and initially motivated or not, whatever their race, ethnicity, age, or gender. There must be not only the perception but the *reality* of fairness and equal access for all employees in an organization.

Programs that are narrowly targeted may cause more employee dissension than growth and development. Noncollege-educated workers constitute the great majority of the workforce, but employability skills are largely left out of their training equation. The fact that only 34 percent of current training dollars go to them severely affects this country's potential to build a workforce that can adapt to change (Tan 1988).

PRINCIPLE 5:
ENGAGE IN PROACTIVE OUTREACH

The most effective employability programs emphasize strong, imaginative outreach activities on the part of managers and program staff to encourage participation. This means more than notices on bulletin boards and stories in the employee newsletter. The outreach must be proactive, direct, and energetic; it must use multiple strategies; and it must employ many advocates. It can include print media, such as posters, notices with paychecks, announcements in company and union newsletters, and letters mailed to employees' homes. It should also include opportunities for employees to meet with management, training providers, or both so they can explain the program and answer questions. Outreach must also include enlisting the support of supervisors and union officials by giving them enough advance information so they will understand and support participation rather than undermine it. Too many organizations have initiated EGDPs whose value seemed to them self-evident, only to be disappointed by a low participation rate when the program was not adequately promoted.

Effective outreach for a program that addresses workers' genuine concerns and to which the organization is commited can lead to participation rates twenty times the 3 to 5 percent average. For example, employee outreach among a major paper company's workers in the forests of the Northeast was carried out primarily by "Dutch," a highly articulate, persuasive, former blue-collar worker who spoke the language of the employees, had had the experience of studying while working full time, understood the dimensions of their work lives, and knew about their need to think ahead to the time when they would be too old to topple big trees and run logs down the river. He went out into the woods to talk with the workers, individually and in groups, donned a hard-hat to ride with them on the big tractors, shared their lunches, and gave them solid reasons for beginning to think about what they might want to do in five, ten, or twenty years. Meanwhile, the program director had gained the cooperation of the workers' team managers, who encouraged their own work teams to participate. Notices were sent out with paychecks three months running, and workshop schedules were not only posted but scheduled by region so that a whole team could attend.

This highly proactive recruitment was so successful that 86 percent of the eligible men and women responded to the initial outreach. Over 80 percent attended the Returning to Learning workshops. This caused a minor scheduling and staffing crisis but ultimately led to a 27 percent enrollment in credit or noncredit courses at a variety of institutions. Actual participation may have been even higher than 27 percent, because some workers simply deferred their use of the education benefits to a more convenient time.

A few corporate partners have agreed to sponsor well-designed, imaginative employability programs but then, to contain costs, have kept participation down by using a restrictive formula or a low-key approach to recruiting. These policies are certainly effective in reducing program costs, but one must wonder what motivated these corporations to initiate the programs in the first place.

PRINCIPLE 6:
PROVIDE PREPAID TUITION

Lack of financial resources is a primary deterrent to participants considering formal learning programs (Darkenwald and Valentine 1985). The most effective employability programs minimize the financial barriers and disincentives to employees. It is preferable that tuition be prepaid by the sponsors, that other normal costs of instruction and support and administrative services do not fall on the learners, that book costs are reimbursed, and that other special costs (e.g., child care) are either covered or made more affordable and accessible for the prospective participants.

If this sounds like an expensive giveaway, consider the alternatives. Many companies have had tuition reimbursement programs in place for years and participation has been minimal, leading the sponsors to conclude that their workers are not interested in furthering their education. Such programs typically require that the employee pay tuition upfront, to be reimbursed upon successful completion of the course. Some companies pay back only a percentage of the tuition based on the grades achieved, a practice that adds a punitive dimension to what is already an economically threatening situation for the worker.

Even if tuition reimbursement is certain, consider the situation of a single mother whose budget simply cannot stretch to cover the $400 for the speedwriting course she needs to remain competitive in her office unless she defers buying new shoes and shirts for her children. Or the father who must choose between taking an accounting course and paying his daughter's orthodontist. It is difficult for a hard-pressed, lower-middle-class family to take the long view of the benefits of training and education when the checkbook is empty and bills are mounting up. The participants' commitment to learning should be measured not in dollars but in the sacrifices they make in their personal lives to succeed.

Prepaid tuition is the key to involving more workers in employability programs. The data supporting this conclusion are dramatic. For example, in the experience of the Mountain Bell/CWA/IBEW PATHWAYS to the Future Program, fewer than 25 percent of nonmanagement personnel used a reimbursement program, but almost 80 percent of them used prepaid tuition (Greenberg 1990). Moreover, employers' fears about having to pay for large numbers of course failures or dropouts have proved unfounded where the counsels and supports of an employability program are also provided. Students who go to school under prepaid tuition plans apparently do not suffer any diminution of will to succeed. In fact, their grades and rates of completion are slightly better than those of employees who must wait for reimbursement.

PRINCIPLE 7: REMOVE INSTITUTIONAL BARRIERS & DISINCENTIVES

Many educational institutions erect or condone barriers and disincentives that have a direct effect on program participation. These barriers may involve inconvenient times and places for classes, lack of access to needed learning resources, or unapproachable, inaccessible instructors, counselors, and essential administrative service officers. Other barriers include obstacles to the fair and full transfer of credit earned elsewhere and severely limited hours for access to essential services such as registration, admissions processes, financial aid information, bill payment, and program advising and planning. Refusal to provide these essential services at more convenient off-site locations is also a disincentive.

Consider the plight of the factory worker who wants to register for a course in mechanical drawing scheduled to begin in two weeks. He must apply for admission, talk to the instructor about whether he has the necessary course prerequisites, register for the course, and buy his books. He leaves his workplace at 4:30 p.m. without stopping to wash up or get a sandwich, drives 30 miles to the campus, and spends about 10 minutes finding a parking place, only to discover that the essential offices close at 5 p.m. and the instructor's posted hours are 10 a.m. to noon on Tuesdays and Thursdays.

Or consider the dilemma of the office secretary who needs a certificate in management information systems (MIS) so she can get the title and salary her current job responsibilities reflect. The only college that has an MIS certificate program is on the other side of town and has no classes that begin later than 5:30 p.m., nor does it offer a weekend program. Even if she could get permission to leave work early, she would have to take four prerequisite courses before entering the program, three of which are in areas in which she has prior college-level learning acquired on the job. The college has no prior learning assessment program through which she can get credit for her learning, so she will have to spend precious time (and company money) to take courses in subjects she already knows before she can take the courses she needs. Finally, in filling out the college registration forms, she must appeal a requirement to get her parent's signature.

Many colleges and universities and most community colleges have already realized that if they wish to serve adult learners, they must remove barriers like these. But old habits die hard. Despite the steadily rising age of learners and the economic incentives for institutions to provide better access for adults, barriers and disincentives still exist. They must be dealt with both in program design and by unremitting pressure from the partners in employability programs.

PRINCIPLE 8: START PRIOR LEARNING ASSESSMENT PROGRAMS

In the past 20 years, a number of postsecondary education institutions have begun to look closely at what people learn outside the classroom. Both research and common sense tell us that nonclassroom (sometimes misnamed experiential) learning is extensive and pervasive throughout the population and is often similar to learning derived from colleges and universities. Through a process called prior learning assessment (PLA), schools have begun to evaluate this "experiential" learning. When they determine it to be similar in content, depth, and breadth to what they teach, they award college credit for it.

PLA is now a recognized academic practice that encompasses a number of evaluative techniques. These include oral and written tests, some nationally standardized; examination of professional and technical apprenticeships, licenses, and other qualifications; performance observation; and product evaluation. Another technique is portfolio-assisted assessment, a process whereby learners compile, define, describe, and document their various learnings in the context of their degree programs and college expectations. The learning attested by these portfolios is then evaluated by faculty, who may recommend college credit for it.

PLA represents a substantial savings of time, money and effort. More significantly, the awards may enhance the student's self-esteem, improving his or her chances of succeeding in further learning experiences. Employability programs should seek as partners education providers who respect extracollegiate learning and are prepared to recognize it formally in an academically responsible fashion. Awarding learner-workers appropriate credit for what they already know gives them a jump-start toward further education and is a powerful predictor of success for all the partners.

PRINCIPLE 9:
PROVIDE WORKPLACE SUPPORT SYSTEMS

The most productive employability programs include strategies designed to make the workplace a more supportive environment and to encourage application of newly acquired skills to the job at hand. It is critical that learners be helped to build their own personal support systems. But support must begin at the worksite — from the employer, the immediate work supervisor, and fellow workers, all of whom may need to be more flexible in their demands and tolerant of behavior that varies from workplace norms. (Stories abound of workers who ridicule fellow workers for reading textbooks during their lunch breaks and of supervisors, apparently resentful of the workers' educational activities, who deliberately reschedule shifts to make it impossible for them to attend class.) If the workforce is unionized, support from the union is also critical. So is support from the worker's spouse and other family members and friends.

The staff of the employability program should include personnel sensitive to these learner-workers' needs and skilled in providing strategies and mechanisms to satisfy them. Some of the support can be provided directly by advisors or counselors, either at work or at school. Their role must be enlarged, however, to encompass not only direct interaction with the learner-workers but also active intervention to change the climate of the workplace so that an employee rushing out after work to the library is hailed rather than ridiculed. This change of climate usually requires support from the highest corporate level as well as immediate supervisors. If training dollars are to have a multiplying effect, an environment must be created that encourages employees to share new learning and skills, as discussed in the next chapter.

PRINCIPLE 10:
ESTABLISH & MAINTAIN GOALS & VALUES

The employability program must be staffed by people who understand and believe deeply in its purpose, philosophy, and espoused values. It must also be served by learning institutions that welcome and accommodate the learner-worker. Giving mere lip service to the program will destroy it. Those involved must practice their values in every aspect of the program, including being open to all, practicing informed advocacy, removing barriers and disincentives, creating support systems, making relevant information readily available, and, above all, respecting the individual learner.

These 10 principles are commonsense ideas that have evolved from many attempts to build employability programs that work. Their presence is no guarantee of success, but their absence is a guarantee of failure. Over the past five years these principles have been validated through trial and error in companies like Bell of Pennsylvania, Scott Paper, Wisconsin Bell, and US WEST Communications; in unions like UAW, IBEW, CWA, and UFCW; in state governments like Indiana and Ohio, Georgia and New York; and in federal government agencies like the departments of Agriculture and Labor. They are the proven keys to greater worker involvement in efforts to achieve employability and to the subsequent upgrading of the skills of the American workforce.

Figure 11.1

WHAT BROKER-MANAGERS OF EMPLOYABILITY PROGRAMS DO

■ Reach out to employers & unions to enlist partners

■ Co-design the programs with other partners

■ Reach out to education & training providers to enlist them, develop capability matrices on them, and brief them on the specifics of participation, payment, etc.

■ Reach out to employees to increase participation

■ Recruit & train provider liaisons

■ Recruit & train career and education counselors for employees

■ Conduct monthly or quarterly meetings for coordination among providers

■ Manage specialized training workshops

■ Provide ongoing service to employees to approve career & education plans, issue letters of credit, approve providers, authorize disbursement of tuition and fee payments, & reimburse costs for books

■ Manage celebratory occasions to honor learners, providers, & other key participants

■ Gather, analyze, & manage data

■ Evaluate programs

■ Generate special programs where requested

■ Provide general administration

USING THE PRINCIPLES IN PRACTICE

It is no easy task to embody all 10 of these principles in a functioning employability program. The most successful programs of which we know have either engaged outside broker-managers for this purpose or have created a special broker-manager of their own. The Big Three automakers and their union partners took the latter course, developing a "jointure" in the form of a non-profit entity to oversee the delivery of their collectively bargained benefits. In some cases this entity has in turn engaged outside help, either for start-up (as with the UAW-Ford National Development and Training Center) or on an ongoing basis (as with US WEST Communications, CWA, and IBEW). Figure 11.1 lists the tasks from among which a particular broker-manager is assigned responsibilities. Small businesses, as noted in Chapter 4, can afford these services only if a consortium of users shares the costs. The stakes — the potential benefits and their costs if not well applied — are so high that, as noted in Chapter 7, we regard provision of this broker-manager service as key to assuring the effectiveness of employability programs.

WORK SETTINGS
AS LEARNING ENVIRONMENTS

Employability, as we have emphasized, requires that workers have the skills to do their jobs, are motivated to use their skills, and work in job settings that encourage continual use and development of their skills. Clearly, employability cannot be achieved through classroom instruction alone. In this chapter we outline ways work settings can be formed into learning environments that improve employability and challenge the sanctity of the classroom as the exclusive arena for developing the employability of the U.S. workforce. We also discuss how work settings as learning environments (WSLEs) support high performance work cycles. The chapter concludes with recommendations for the roles regulatory agencies, colleges, and labor unions can play in supporting the ideas presented in this chapter.

DEVELOPING SKILLS ON THE JOB

The importance of a job environment in developing employability skills is continually evident in the research. For example, Morrison and Brantner (1992), in a comprehensive path analysis of 53 variables, found that the rate individuals acquired proficiency in a new job depended in large part on (1) their own level of self-efficacy; (2) length of time in the job; and (3) a supportive work environment that provided clear roles, cooperation from their supervisors, the time and resources for learning the job, and tasks that their supervisors indicated were important to the organization. In this study, previous classroom education and technical training experience did not contribute significantly to learning how to do a new job.

Surprisingly, Morrison and Brantner found that prior experience in related job areas was a deterrent to learning a new job. Individuals actually learned new skills most quickly when they had little or no prior experience in a job because counter-productive habits and misconceptions picked up through previous experience had to be "unlearned" before new skills could be acquired. We have encountered this phenomenon in our own experiences.

For example, one organization we worked with had great difficulty setting up a WSLE because the project team comprised staff development specialists with a long history of conducting classroom training. We spent the first three months working through resistance like *"I simply don't believe that we can do this training in any way but through the tried and true classroom methods."* As the staff "relearned" what a comprehensive training strategy included, the project began to move forward. In contrast, a group of engineers with little prior experience in training easily rejected a classroom model and set up a process that imbedded customer service training in the actual jobs of project managers. Because of the possible contaminating influence of prior experiences, efforts to set up WSLEs must support both unlearning and relearning.

Another component of a work setting as a learning environment is high learning expectations set by the supervisor. The research of Locke and Latham (1990) suggests that supervisors who set specific, difficult learning goals will stimulate higher learning performance than supervisors who set easy goals, vague goals such as "do your best," or no goals at all. A surprising finding of their research was that *"assigning [learning] goals to individuals generally leads to the same level of commitment and performance as letting individuals participate in the setting of their goals or letting them set their own goals"* (241). Workers can interpret the assignment of learning goals as a challenge to take on new job tasks to prove their competence. Because individuals in a job setting receive feedback about their work and learning from many sources (co-workers, customers, friends), feedback from supervisors on specific learning goals helps workers to assess their own accomplishments (Locke and Latham 1990).

Supervisors can also establish work settings as learning environments by emphasizing collaborative or team learning activities. When learning can help solve a frustrating work problem that affects an entire group, the personal sense of pride at mastering a challenging situation is reinforced by co-workers' professional recognition for a job well done (Millis 1992). Collective learning efforts also contribute to individual development because each time individuals work through a problem with co-workers, their knowledge about their job and their understanding of how it relates to the organization increase (Lindsey, Homes, and McCall, 1987). Additionally, the process of performing any aspect of a job creates, in and of itself, new knowledge about how to do the job. When individuals work collaboratively with others, the personal insights they conceive through the experience are sources of new learning for co-workers.

SUPERVISORS AS INSTRUCTORS

Supervisors and managers are frequently reluctant to support work settings as learning environments. They ask: *"What skills would I teach that they couldn't get from a better source?"* The supervisor's role as instructor is to help workers understand complex organizational relationships that are important for employability. Most workers understand the abstract meaning of terms like "profit" or "total quality," but they do not always know how to use these abstract notions in business practices.

Supervisors can use their understanding of organizational relationships to guide discussions so workers understand why certain ideas, suggestions, or proposals are more appropriate than others. In this way, supervisors can advance the employability skills of their supervisees in areas such as planning and allocating resources, participating as members of teams, or acquiring and evaluating information.

In many firms that are adopting total quality management practices, the supervisor-as-teacher continually helps workers refine their understanding of "total quality" and its meaning for day-to-day business practices. For example, one business used its total quality emphasis on measurable goals to create an excellent learning environment. When project teams tracked quality ratios, such as "total deliveries on time divided by total deliveries," supervisors-as-teachers stimulated discussions at project review meetings on how the ratios could be improved during the next project cycle. Thus, the supervisors-as-teachers established an ongoing learning process that helped to improve the employability and productivity skills of the workers involved.

In summary, work settings as learning environments that cultivate employability skills have specific characteristics:

- Supervisors are competent and use a cooperative leadership style.

- Supervisors provide clear job and role expectations.

- Supervisors emphasize that performance of job roles is important.

- The organizational pace of activity allows reasonable time for doing the job and for professional development.

- The employability skills being developed are actually used within the organization's current operations.

- Supervisors communicate high expectations for learning.

- A collaborative learning process is used.

■ Workers are given guidance in unlearning old, counter-productive habits.

■ Individuals are assigned to jobs for a long enough time to learn them (Lindsey, Homes, and McCall 1987; Locke and Latham 1990; Millis 1992; Morrison and Brantner 1992).

THE ROLE OF CLASSROOM PROGRAMS

Employee growth and development programs, as described in Chapter 11, provide the availability and access to instructional resources needed to develop employability. Work environments that successfully develop employability complement EGDPs by ensuring long-term availability of and access to EGDP resources. Workers are not limited to one-day discussions of techniques, content, or skills. Nor is development of their employability restricted to completion of a one-semester course, a single academic degree, or a professional seminar series. In an ideal scenario, EDGP resources are used throughout a career to develop, augment, and refine baseline employability skills.

In the usual training situation, as pictured in Figure 12.1, a short-term session achieves demonstrated growth in principles, techniques, or skills. Each time the work setting fails to support the new skill, or the employee has difficulty using the principles, a degree of the learning evaporates.

But when the organization gives the development of employability a long-term focus, ideas for improving business practices that are formed in classroom programs continue to grow. In a WSLE, with the collaborative support of supervisors and co-workers, a worker's long-term learning process is never completed. Each application of a skill learned in a classroom leads to a new set of possibilities that, in turn, promote second and third generations of applications.

In one organization where learning a new computer-based accounting system was designed as a long-term process, data-entry clerks developed so many new uses of the computer system that their trainers asked them, just three months after the initial training sessions, to work as consultants on how the computer system could be used in another agency. In this WSLE, after only a short period the students knew more about the system's applications than did their teachers.

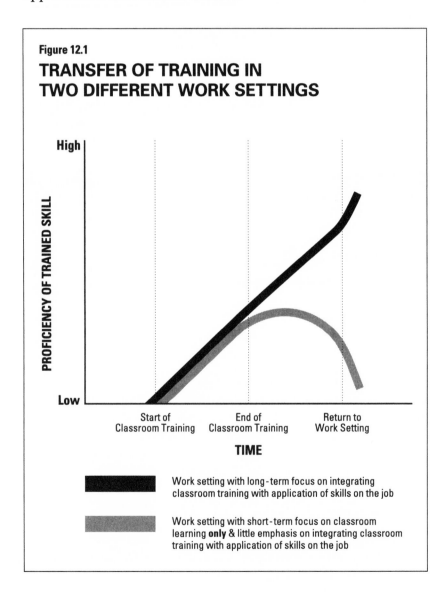

Figure 12.1

TRANSFER OF TRAINING IN
TWO DIFFERENT WORK SETTINGS

Work setting with long-term focus on integrating classroom training with application of skills on the job

Work setting with short-term focus on classroom learning **only** & little emphasis on integrating classroom training with application of skills on the job

Cultivating the requisite skills for lifelong employability in classroom settings requires appropriate methods. As discussed in Chapter 8, research indicates that adults learn best when the teaching process makes connections with the real world, allows group interaction, provides prompt feedback, communicates high expectations, and respects diverse talents and ways of learning (Chickering and Gamson 1987).

Skill development also depends on training programs that match the level of instruction with the learner's level of expertise.

THE CONTINUUM OF COMPETENCE

Research on the development of professional competence depicts a novice-to-expert continuum (Dreyfus and Dreyfus 1986). As outlined in Figure 12.2, the greatest difference between novices and experts is how they think while doing their jobs. Novices tend to think in black and white terms. Regardless of the situation, they follow rules set forth in manuals. In contrast, experts think intuitively and holistically. Where novices focus on basic rules and procedures, experts visualize holistic patterns. Along the continuum separating novices from experts, there are many important differences in how workers think while doing their job. For example, advanced beginners can distinguish situations calling for exceptions to rules. Practitioners combine exceptions to rules into general principles. Professionals combine general principles into broader, more intuitive patterns to guide their actions.

These differences have important implications for skill development. Usually training, education, and professional development activities concentrate on imparting basic rules and procedures at the novice level. Little attention is paid to the developmental importance of challenging workers to appreciate exceptions to the rules, formulate guiding principles, construct holistic strategies, or refine intuitions. Most employees at the expert end of the continuum are trained as if they were novices.

Figure 12.2

THE CONTINUUM OF COMPETENCE

Level of Competence	Description	Rules vs. Situation	Learning Emphasis
NOVICE	Analytical; no perspective; detached from situation	Rules are applied without consideration of context	Learn basic rules & procedures as outlined in book/manual
ADVANCED BEGINNER	Analytical; no perspective; involved in situation but decision is detached	Rules have exceptions in particular situations	Aspects of a situation requiring an adaptation of rules
PRACTITIONER	Analytical; chooses a perspective; decision is detached but person is involved in outcome	Rules follow general principles that apply to a wide range of situations	General principles that apply to a wide range of situations
PROFESSIONAL	Analytical; experience provides a perspective; decision is detached; person is involved in understanding	Rules & general principles are tempered by experience	Overall patterns based on experience Images & intuitions that inform integrated holistic behavior
EXPERT	Intuitive; experience provides a perspective; person is involved in decision *and* outcome	Rules, principles, actions & outcomes are fit together like a hand & glove	Involves integration of actions principles, & outcomes

Adapted from Dreyfus & Dreyfus 1986

They are seldom placed in learning situations that challenge them to test and refine the intuitions they use to guide their decisions.

A company committed to maximizing the learning potential of the work setting will design training and development activities along a novice to expert continuum. For example, one organization used this approach to improve its project managers' ability to select quality vendors. Since each project manager in this case was experienced and knowledgeable about the black and white policies and about procedures regarding vendor relationships, another workshop on quality vendors would not have been useful. Instead, the company scheduled an all-day discussion among project managers to identify and agree upon criteria to select quality vendors. During the session, project managers subjected the personal intuitions that guided their decisions to the scrutiny of other project managers. Through the exchange and discussion of ideas, project managers refined their approaches to exercising vendor options and developed valuable guidelines for future decisions.

When the participants first looked at the agenda, several asked, *"Why are you calling this a training session? No one is giving us a lecture."* But by the end of the day, the participants judged that the new ideas, insights, and perspectives they had learned from their colleagues were invaluable. This outcome was achieved by matching the focus of the instruction with the participants' level of expertise.

LIMITATIONS OF CLASSROOM TRAINING

A bias toward classroom training is strongly entrenched in many strategies proposed to increase employability. For example, to develop needed employability skills among workers, the recent SCANS conference report (Department of Labor 1991) recommends a traditional classroom-based model, even though studies on how workers develop competencies show that classroom-based programs do not develop desired workplace skills.

Research indicates that the exclusive use of classroom-based instruction may be one reason for the ineffectiveness of many past employability programs. According to Dertouzos, Lester, and Solow (1989), too many graduates of educational and vocational classroom programs have difficulty with job situations requiring them to allocate resources suitably, relate well interpersonally, use information appropriately, work productively with technologies, or successfully improve complex organizational systems. Based on a review of the literature on transfer of learning, Laker (1990) determined that most learners fail to apply in the workplace the skills, abilities, and knowledge they acquire during classroom training sessions.

In their study of how executives developed leadership qualities like negotiating skills, Lindsey, Homes, and McCall (1987) concluded that classroom training was not a robust influence on learning job skills. Their study confirmed that nonclassroom experiences such as starting a new project from scratch and influence from bosses or mentors were the most potent events in developing leadership capabilities. Of the 35 leadership competencies they studied, classroom training contributed to only five — among them specific technical knowledge, perspectives for framing problems, and management models and theories. The remaining 30 leadership skills — such as getting cooperation, influencing others, and understanding complex relationships — were developed through actual job assignments.

Achieving employability of the workforce requires a spectrum of approaches. WSLEs are necessary to both complement and supplement classroom programs.

ACHIEVING HIGH PERFORMANCE

Development of employability skills depends on a complementary interaction between classroom programs and work settings that serve as learning environments (Figure 12.3). Employability skills, in turn, enable workers to do their jobs in a way that

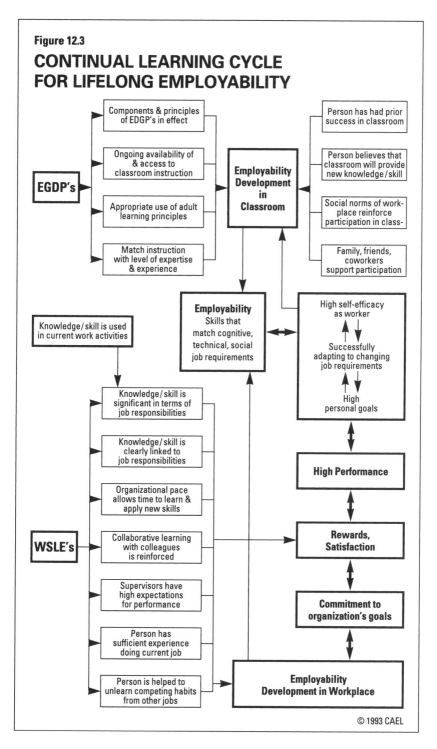

Figure 12.3

CONTINUAL LEARNING CYCLE FOR LIFELONG EMPLOYABILITY

© 1993 CAEL

183

increases self-efficacy and helps them attain personal goals. When a job is accomplished in this manner, high performance results (Bandura 1982). Through high performance, workers experience rewards and personal satisfaction and commit to future high performance goals (Locke and Latham 1990).

Chapter 1 outlined how Joan developed her employability skills. As you may recall, Joan was assigned to a cellular manufacturing unit within her company that had all the characteristics of a high performance work setting. In a cooperative manner, her supervisor set performance goals and provided clear role assignments. Within the cellular unit, the set-up and assembly procedures Joan learned and refined were reinforced as significant aspects of the organization's current business cycle. The steady work pace of the unit allowed her to do her job and collaborate with co-workers on ways to continually improve set-up and assembly procedures. Team discussions led by her supervisor helped clarify how her day-to-day work fit in with the overall total quality goals of the organization.

In this setting Joan learned the employability skills of group effectiveness, personal management, adaptability, influence, communication, competence, and knowing how to learn outlined in Chapter 6. Equipped with these skills, Joan is a high performance worker. When she uses these skills to accomplish a challenging job task or solve perplexing problems, her sense of competence and self-efficacy increases. Her personal goals, in turn, expand as she sees herself capable and able to take on more complex work assignments.

According to Locke and Latham (1990), Joan's successful completion of a challenging job task in this particular WSLE sets up a continual high performance work cycle. Joan's success begets more success. When her performance meets or exceeds her supervisor's standards, her rewarding sense of pride, satisfaction, and accomplishment can result in a progressive adjustment of personal goals to take on similar or more difficult tasks that, when successfully accomplished, will result in more pride and satisfaction. Joan is likely to continue this cycle because in this job setting she can perform a variety of tasks, receives direct feedback from her supervisor, has responsibility and autonomy for her work, can identify with a final product, and feels that her work is significant. People experience the greatest satisfaction from their work when it includes these five characteristics (Hackman and Oldman 1980).

When Joan experiences these rewards and satisfaction from her high performance work, she is further inclined to develop her employability skills. Her expanded commitment to organizational goals will result in more learning efforts within her cellular unit. As a result of her increasing sense of self-confidence, she will more likely take advantage of formal educational opportunities to increase her employability skills — particularly if her company adopts an employee growth and development program.

One business leader who reviewed this manuscript noted skeptically that workers like Joan do not exist. The idealized workplace learning process we outline here is, in his view, rare. We agree. Joan's case is, unfortunately, an exception. There are too few organizations (with businesses like Chaparral Steel among the noted exceptions) that make a serious commitment to workers like Joan and establish a work setting that develops employability skills and supports their use in a high performance enterprise. With research studies and a few shining examples supporting us, we hope that more businesses will enter into partnerships with unions and workers to transform business settings into continuously improving learning organizations. In the most productive companies, learning never ends and expertise is developed continually. When the learning potential of the workplace is maximized, learning becomes coterminous with work.

PARTNERSHIP ROLES

To achieve the full learning possibilities of the workplace as a learning environment several changes will be necessary. First, regulatory agencies will have to increase the flexibility of their certification procedures. For example, one service agency attempted to install this workplace learning process to improve its stagnant staff development program. The program was halted at the starting gate by a regulatory agency's rigid requirement that the times, dates, places, lesson plans, and attendance rosters for all training sessions be on file. If these documents were not in place when regulators reviewed a service site, the regulators would conclude that required training had not occurred and would revoke staff licenses. The enforcers held to this position publicly even though they privately acknowledged that the traditional workshops they required had little impact on client services.

Second, educational institutions will have to relinquish their near monopoly on certification credentials. Right now the educational sector dictates many of the activities and most of the processes required to achieve employability credentials. When WSLEs are included in developing employability skills, educational institutions will have to enter into alliances with, or relinquish control to, businesses and unions. The apprenticeship process, for example, is one area where this partnership is working.

Labor unions should become advocates within the learning enterprise on behalf of their members. By maximizing the learning potential of the workplace, unions could promise cross-training and multiple learning options that would enhance the lifelong employability of their members. In this new role, abor unions would become central agents in the learning enterprise and might administer a variety of credentials and certificates themselves. They could shift from their current focus on situational job security to a pattern of lifelong employability for all members.

In the end, workers will benefit from the transformation of the workplace to a learning and producing environment. A system that maximizes the learning opportunities of the workplace will eradicate some of the problems of access that are barriers to many learners. When a new set of credentials based on workplace learning options is in place, the career mobility and life-long employability of all workers will be greatly enhanced.

13

TOWARD A NATIONAL POLICY

A number of difficult changes must occur to achieve near-universal employability of the U.S. workforce and the productivity it can provide:

- Expanded and changing learning programs and providers to accommodate a doubled or tripled level of adult learning activity (see Chapters 6 and 9);

- A functioning economy with an increasing array of high performance work organizations with customers for its products and services, with jobs that pay living wages, and with efficient production and a work environment congenial to learning on the job (see Chapter 7);

- A workforce that can perform the jobs suited to the niches in the world economy that the U.S. economy can fill (see Chapters 8 and 9);

- Capabilities for bringing together the partners critical to implementing EGDPs, identifying current and long-range training and education needs, and brokering and managing these endeavors (discussed in Part 2, especially Chapter 7);

- Financing for the education and training needed for universal employability and incentives and controls for their fair and efficient use;

■ Coalitions of advocates and watchdogs to provide appropriate voice and clout for consumers, workers, and small businesses (see Chapters 4, 5, 9 and 10);

■ Resources and institutions to carry out a program of research and technical services (briefly discussed in Chapter 7);

■ Strategies and programs for preventing or overcoming self-compounding disadvantages for component groups within the workforce (see Chapter 10);

■ An overarching vision, with implementing policies, regulation, management, and evaluation of the employability effort as a whole.

Four issues are central to national employability: overall vision and governing policies, financing, effective coordination of partners' efforts, and incentives for ongoing energetic cooperation. These four concerns constitute the agenda for this final chapter.

A VISION OF NEAR-UNIVERSAL EMPLOYABILITY

Many industry and labor leaders, educators, and public policy-makers would doubtless agree that greater investment in people's qualifications for work is critically needed. But the United States does not yet in practice treat human resource development as a priority issue of public policy (Miller 1989). Neither the executive nor the legislative branch of the federal government has a coherent policy for it. Education providers are as divided on these issues as they are diverse in their missions and financing. There is no arena in which the various essential partners in employability development are working together to define key issues and iron out differences.

Our vision is that a means be found to treat human resource development among the American people as one integrated effort and to give this effort as high a priority as any other issue of contemporary public policy. This is not to suggest that the federal government alone should define or administer such policy. The task of optimizing the qualifications and the productivity of the workforce should instead be seen as a collaborative effort. All partners must see this responsibility as a complex one. They must interact constantly while keeping their focus on achieving a fully employable workforce.

To complement the collaboration of leaders, the vision calls for a spotlight on the individual worker's responsibility. Each worker's development of his or her own capabilities is a learning and growing process that must continue throughout life. While help is of course required at times, the goal is for each worker to manage his or her own development and employability.

PUBLIC POLICY

One element of an adequate public policy on human resource development is the commitment of the responsible authorities to weigh and evaluate policies about any part of the nation's learning system in terms of their effects on the other parts of the system and on the system as a whole in furthering the goal of an employable workforce. For example, Congress currently legislates about higher education in one set of measures, corporate training in another, and elementary and secondary education in still a third. It also enacts in its diverse welfare, unemployment, and other social policies provisions that restrict or regulate the use of education providers — all without adequate attention to the impact of one set of laws on the others. On many of these issues, the states also legislate and create systems for implementation that lack coordination or even compatibility. What is needed is, in a manner of speaking, an environmental impact study before such measures are enacted. That is, the impact of each on the others must be known before lawmakers weigh what to do (Kernan-Schloss 1989).

A further element of national policy on workforce employability should be the premise that the legitimate vehicles for teaching what workers need to know include not only the public and private nonprofit schools, colleges, and universities but also corporate training facilities, apprenticeships, union-sponsored programs for worker education and training, proprietary schools, educational telecommunications, museum and library education services, other community education provisions, and learner-managed, informal learning activities. Currently, the competing providers of training and education are well aware of their competition and of the diverse kinds of services wanted. But the policies are not in place to assure fair and energetic competition. Both education providers and the users of their services must have an appropriate voice in the ongoing debate as to what the rules of competition should be and how to establish and sustain a joint commitment to the goal of employability. One essential goal of the employability effort is the coinage of accepted credentials of all learning, however and wherever acquired. The policies and practices necessary for assessing and evaluating learning have been established through the work of CAEL and the American Council on Education for well over a decade. Lacking is a coherent national system for transferring, banking, and calibrating credit awards and other forms of recognition (see Chapter 9).

It is widely argued that the U.S. educational effort is basically a "nonsystem" that decentralizes the responsibility for education to the states and within them to local boards of education and to competing institutions at every level from preschool through postdoctoral study. Yet the United States is not entirely without governing educational policies. There are, for example, federal policies regarding nondiscrimination on the basis of race, gender, age, religion, or certain handicaps. There are also federal policies relating to finance and financial aid. Accrediting policies and their enforcing bodies introduce a further level of guidance and control. And regulations of such agencies as the Federal Trade Commission deal with everything from truth in advertising to measures aimed at closing down "degree mills."

There are also regulations on the rights of privacy for academic and personnel records, accounting on costs of research, and the taxability of moneymaking enterprises within institutions of higher education.

So the American commitment to decentralization, competition, and academic freedom in educational matters does not preclude governing policies for a national effort in human resource development. We now grasp the need for national goals as to educational attainment, even though the responsibility for achieving them may lie primarily with state or local or multijurisdictional entities such as business corporations. These policies need greater integration if we are to have a fully employable workforce and an educated citizenry.

But how might such goals be articulated? The example of recent leadership, primarily governors, in articulating national goals for elementary and secondary education is a promising precedent. Would it not be timely for the governors, again in cooperation with leaders of the executive and legislative branches of federal government and with representatives of the corporate, labor, and education sectors, to discuss challenging and feasible goals for upgrading the qualifications of the workforce? Leadership on the part of governors need not preclude private efforts of think tanks and individual scholars or innovators to nominate goals and make the case for their particular visions. In fact, gubernatorial support for the task might be an incentive for such groups to tackle the task energetically and promptly.

Past efforts at reform of education have tended to focus almost entirely on children and youth and on precollegiate education. It is a new phenomenon that the overwhelmingly greatest need for learning, quantitatively speaking, is among those already in the workforce (Commission on Higher Education and the Adult Learner 1984). National policy needs to focus enough of the educational establishment's efforts on this new majority of adult learners.

DEFINING EMPLOYABILITY

A national consensus on the vision of human resource development and the elements of policy would help to define the ideal of an employable workforce. Unemployment in the United States reached the level of 7.9 percent of the workforce in January 1993. The number of people drawing unemployment benefits was at a high for the last decade even though the number of employed people had hit an all-time high of over 125 million. The ideal of employability is that all but the most severely and permanently disabled (probably 2 percent or less of the workforce) would be qualified for currently available jobs up to the number of such jobs available.

As discussed previously, employability does not mean that all workers will be continuously employed, since fluctuations occur in the total number of jobs available, the supply of workers, and mismatches between worker and job. Reaching the ideal of capacity for work inherent in the notion of a fully employable workforce would mean, however, a significantly lower net unemployment rate than we have in early 1993. The most radical change will not be in the numbers but in the level and variety of qualifications the workforce will provide and the speed at which this human resource bank will grow.

For the workforce of the United States to have the qualifications we have sketched and the capability for continuing improvement, its education and training activity will need to double or triple in size and to be better distributed among (1) worksites designed as learning environments (which must grow), (2) formal in-house education and training (which will probably grow), (3) formal outsourced education and training (which may or may not grow), and (4) individually chosen continuing learning in formal and informal settings. These four arenas of adult learning will compete for the individual's time. The first two will have the advantage in that they can occur on paid work time, without competing with other demands on the adult worker's time. At the same time, the pressure for businesses to be efficient, the rapid changes in education and training needs, and the fact that public education providers are subsidized where in-house training is not may cause employers to "buy" a larger proportion of education and training from these public providers than they currently do.

Given the causal connection between appropriate qualifications and productivity in work and the link between productivity and competitiveness of enterprise, the pressure for learning to be efficient will rise. Learners will have to gain knowledge and competence more quickly than before and learning facilitators (in-house training programs, external educational and training institutions) will have to adopt strategies and tools that foster learning efficiency. The degree of efficiency achieved could have a major impact on the costs of acquiring the needed capabilities and knowledge. The accountability movement currently in vogue will be accentuated as it applies to the cost effectiveness of education and training with the active workforce.

The learning most needed in this employability effort will involve not simply the acquisition of knowledge but also its application to problems and issues in the workplace. The worker who has mastered this kind of learning will be in high demand. The education enterprise will most likely be required to adapt its current philosophy and offerings to give greater weight to developing people capable of meeting employer requirements and sustaining lifelong employability. Whether this learning will have the prestige prized within higher education and in the broader public's pecking order of credentials is less clear.

EFFECTS ON HUMAN RESOURCE DEVELOPMENT

Once this vision is adopted and the policies essential to it are in place, the human resource development system will accelerate by virtue of its own internal dynamics. The weight of evidence suggests that there will continue to be greater movement among career lines within a lifetime, in part because the work life of the average worker will continue to lengthen. Pressures to continue working rather than retire early may increase as the tax-supported costs of entitlement programs continue to escalate. In addition, if workers enhance their qualifications at the level of generic capabilities and not just job-specific skills, their opportunities for rewarding changes of career are likely to grow.

Countering these forces toward greater mobility among jobs and careers will be growing employer efforts to retain productive workers and to provide them variety and advancement within the same firm. In any case, the more diversely and highly qualified workers are, the more free they will be to move or stay put. The tension between capable workers seeking places to exercise their skills and employers obligating skilled workers with developmental opportunities will fuel an escalating skill-development cycle that will counter the low skills/low wages philosophy currently dominating American business.

FINANCING A NATIONWIDE EMPLOYABILITY PROGRAM

If the articulation of national goals and policies on employability is to be a coalition effort led by influentials among the essential partners, and if the key policy agenda is as we have described, how can the effort be financed? What are the primary cost components? Where, in these times of national debt and tax resistance, are the resources to be found?

First, what needs financing is essentially the doubling or tripling of the effectiveness of the training and education of the workforce. Doubling the effect does not mean doubling the cost, since (as already noted) substantial efficiencies are feasible. If a major part of corporate training effectiveness is lost (Georgenson 1982) because of learning lost in the transfer to application, fixing this flaw can recoup much of the cost of a better effort. (The strategies for accomplishing this task are outlined in Chapter 12.)

Adequate financing will require widespread participation by employers as well as ongoing contributions by workers and taxpayers. The costs to be funded include much more than the outright education and training costs. Related costs spring from regulation of the expanded learning system, prevention and control of fraud and abuse, coordination of efforts in both policy development and implementation, development of nationwide or state-by-state credentialing systems, and tax exemptions used as incentives for workforce participation. One way to envisage the cost sharing needed to cover these expenses is to outline the potential contributions of the different partners and the sources of their respective contributions.

From employers:

■ At least 1.5 percent of payroll dedicated to training and education of employees, via a mandated national tax, forgivable if the corporation spends the required amounts on its own workforce;[1]

■ Continuing in-house training specific to company priorities;

■ Provision of related services typical of the CAEL-managed employee growth and development programs;

■ A commitment to maximizing the learning potential of their own work settings; and

■ Investment of a significantly higher percentage of payroll costs in training and education.

These contributions would be financed by the current employer-sponsored fringe-benefit programs plus the federally mandated training contributions. They would be offset in part by savings from less waste in the transfer of training to application on the job and in part by higher prices for products and services.

---

1. The current percentage is only 1.3 percent of payroll (Dole 1989). On European practices, see Lynton 1992.

From workers and their unions:

■ Workers' acceptance of lifelong responsibility for their own knowledge and skill development and unions' making it a priority to support this commitment;

■ A share of the costs of tuitions beyond certain levels;

■ Learning on the workers' own time; and

■ Trade-offs of some other fringe benefits for the EGDP benefits.

These contributions come in part from time otherwise devoted to cherished family, community, and leisure activities and in part from compensation that might otherwise be realized. A small part of these costs (tuition share) would also come from cash earnings otherwise spent elsewhere.

From state governments:

■ Exemption of education benefits from taxation;

■ Payment for information services on the capabilities and services of education and training providers and for help for workers in evaluating educational alternatives;

■ Payment of the costs of monitoring the performance of education and training providers;

■ Incentives to employers to exceed the minimum required investment in training;

■ Continued investment in economic development within each state;

■ Modeling of good employer practices in provision of benefits for employees and in efficient use of in-house and outsourced training and education;

■ Adoption of funding formulas for higher education that are more appropriate for the support of part-time learners than awards based on full-time equivalency;

■ Provision of support for colleges' participation in employability partnerships with employers and unions; and

■ Development of coherent statewide employability policies
and programs.

These contributions would be financed (as detailed in Chapter 7)
largely by gains in the productivity of the state economy and
resulting growth in tax base and tax revenues. Payment would
also come from savings from coordination of existing state programs for workforce training and reduction of the costs of welfare,
unemployment, crime, and health care.

From the federal government:

■ Costs of orchestrating policy development;

■ Adoption of a concept of education and training that includes
nonclassroom activities (as outlined in Chapter 12);

■ Exemption of education benefits from taxation;

■ Funding of innovative experiments in employability
(welfare-to-school-to-work ventures, such as America Works
and Dusco Community Services), with incentives for states
to invest in such ventures as well;

■ Removal of barriers to employability, such as barriers to
college study for people on welfare and unfair policies on
financial aid;

■ Removal of all discrimination against older learners and
workforce learners, especially as part-time students;

■ Regulation of training and education agencies (a current
cost, perhaps expanded with the growth of the workforce
development effort); and

■ Research on workforce development.

As detailed in Chapter 7, these contributions would be funded in
part by the increased tax receipts derived from economic growth.

They would also be funded by reductions in the costs of welfare, unemployment, crime, and delinquency and in slower increases in health-care costs.

From philanthropies:

■ Funding of innovative experiments designed to enhance employability;

■ Contributions to financial aid for workforce learners; and

■ Research on workforce development, including the orchestration of its financing.

To make these contributions, foundations would need to subordinate other funding priorities that they see as less beneficial to American society in the long run.

COORDINATING PARTNER EFFORTS & INCENTIVES FOR COOPERATION

At various points throughout this book, we have spelled out in great detail the need for collaboration among diverse partners and for effective coordination of their efforts. Thus far, such cooperation has occurred on a much smaller scale than required for a nationwide employability effort. Most of that effort has been among Fortune 500 corporations and, where organized, their unions. The added effort called for is in enlisting tens of thousands of additional employers, the organized labor movement, and state and federal governments. Brokers, researchers, and support agencies will also need assistance in playing their respective parts.

Current work is focused on developing model statewide employability and productivity programs. Such efforts are almost inevitably led by a statewide council or board with representation from all key stakeholders. Eventually, the authors believe, an analogous coordinating mechanism will be needed at a national level, not to replace the state councils but to complement, support, and coordinate their efforts.

Such a "national employability council" will deal with policy and operational matters. Its agenda will range from entitlements for training and education to regulation of fraud and abuse to incentives for cooperation and assurance of a relatively level playing field among competitors in the diverse forms of service required for this complex undertaking. This council would in some respects be analogous to the Federal Reserve Board or the Tennessee Valley Authority. It would be a quasigovernmental body created by concurrence of the Congress and the President, answering both to them and to the governors of the states, yet free to operate with substantial autonomy within the legislation and funding provided by the government and other stakeholders.

The task of sustaining incentives for all essential partners may require leadership from such a national employability council even though (or because) it will not be able to mandate all of the incentives. The benefits available to all of the partners through active cooperation must be widely publicized and the appeal to both their self-interest and the public interest forcefully stated. Motivating small business owners to cooperate may require special assistance and incentives from state and federal authorities or from regional and local associations of businesses. But for all that a national council can do, the various partners themselves are in position to provide the primary incentives for their counterparts. After a few years of experience with a national employability effort, these partners will be further needed to evaluate and amend the distribution of costs and benefits to sustain a consensus about affordability and fairness.[2]

While this task of coordination, incentive building, and leadership does not have the inherent drama of Star Wars, interplanetary travel, or gene mapping, we recommend it as a

---

[2]. On strategies for interdependence, a mix of which is recommended here, see Cervero 1992.

challenge worthy of the leadership capabilities of contemporary Americans. Indeed, the capacity of the United States to cope with the challenge of universal employability may spell the difference between our continuing to be a leading political and economic power or declining to the status of a tired, second-rank nation whose glory is past.

WHAT IS CAEL?

The Council for Adult and Experiential Learning (CAEL) began in 1974 as a research project of Educational Testing Service and 10 pioneering colleges and universities. The project's purpose was to answer the question, *"Is it possible to do valid and reliable assessment of college-level learning gained from work or life experience?"* The answer to that question, after three years of applied research, was an overwhelming yes. CAEL was incorporated in 1977 as an independent, nonprofit association to promote the concept of prior learning assessment, to develop methods for assessment, to train faculties in assessment methodologies, and to provide publications and other support services to individual adults.

In 1984, CAEL began to work directly with business and organized labor to assist individuals who wished to return to formal learning. These joint ventures have been enormously successful in encouraging adults to return to some kind of further learning, whether in literacy improvement courses, technical or vocational training, or collegiate programs. Workers learn on their own time by attending any one of a network of schools, typically in their immediate geographic area. In a comprehensive joint venture, CAEL provides the following services:

■ Program design and management;

■ Outreach to the workforce in the form of training and workshops;

■ Access to a network of education providers;

■ Employee services, including Returning to Learning® workshops and individualized career and education counseling; and

■ Employee tracking, data processing, and reporting.

Since 1984, CAEL has worked with over 30 corporations, labor unions, and government entities to provide joint venture services to their employees. These experiences contributed directly to *Employability in a High Performance Economy.*

CAEL's mission is to expand lifelong learning opportunities for adults and to advance experiential learning and its assessment. To fulfill that mission, CAEL uses the following strategies:

■ It empowers adults to overcome attitudinal and institutional barriers and to return to learning.

■ It works with educational institutions to develop, improve, and evaluate programs for the assessment of prior learning and other programs and services that are responsive to adult learners.

■ It works with business/industry, labor, and government to develop, implement, and manage programs through which employees can return to learning for personal and professional growth.

■ It contributes to the professional development of practitioners of adult programs.

■ It develops publications and sponsors research, conferences, institutes, and workshops on adult development and adult learning.

■ It seeks to foster change in policies affecting adult learners through collaborative programs with business, labor, education, and government.

■ It cooperates and collaborates with other associations and organizations, as appropriate, to achieve its mission.

CAEL is a membership organization with hundreds of members — including institutions, organizations, businesses, labor unions, and individual members. CAEL maintains four offices: the National Headquarters in Chicago, and regional offices in Cleveland, Denver and Philadelphia.

For further information on CAEL and its work, please write to the National Headquarters at 223 West Jackson Boulevard, Suite 510, Chicago, IL 60606.

BIBLIOGRAPHY

Baldwin, T.T., and Ford, J.K. (1988). Transfer of training: A review and directions for further research. *Personnel Psychology* 41: 63-105.

Bandura, A. (1982). Self-efficacy in human agency. *American Psychologist* 37: 122-147.

Brand, B. (1993). *Here is what we must do at school to get our students ready for work.* Washington, DC: U.S. Department of Education.

Brock, W., and Marshall, M. (1990). Speeches delivered at Conference on the Skills of the American Workforce. New York City.

Brookfield, S.D. (1986). *Understanding and facilitating adult learning.* San Francisco: Jossey-Bass.

Candy, P.C. (1991). *Self-direction for lifelong learning.* San Francisco: Jossey-Bass.

Carnegie Council on Policy Studies in Higher Education (1980). *Three thousand futures: The next twenty years in higher education.* San Francisco: Jossey-Bass.

Carnevale, A.P. (1991). *America and the new economy.* San Francisco: Jossey-Bass.

—. (1982). *Human capital: A high-yield corporate investment.* Washington, DC: American Society for Training and Development.

—. (1986). The learning enterprise. *ASTD Training and Development Journal,* January, 18-26.

—, Gainer, L.J., and Meltzer, A.S. (1990). *Workplace basics: The skills employers want.* Washington, DC: ASTD and U.S. Department of Labor.

Cervero, R.M. (1992). Cooperation and collaboration in the field of continuing professional education. In Hunt, E.S. (ed.) *Professional workers as learners*. Washington, DC: Department of Education, Office of Educational Research and Information (Document #065-000-0531-0).

Charner, I., Knox, K., LeBel, A., Levine, H., Russell, L., and Shore, J. (1978). *An untapped resource: Negotiated tuition-aid in the private sector*. Washington, DC: National Manpower Institute.

Chickering, A.W. (1991). Classroom teaching, personal development and professional competence. In Lamdin, L. (ed.) *Roads to the learning society*. Chicago: CAEL.

— and Gamson, Z. (1987). *Seven principles for good practice in undergraduate education*. Racine, WI: The Johnson Foundation.

College Entrance Examination Board (1988). *How Americans in transition study for college credit*. New York: College Board.

Commission on Higher Education and the Adult Learner (1984). *Adult learners: Key to the nation's future*. Columbia, MD: Commission on Higher Education and the Adult Learner.

Commission on the Skills of the American Workforce (1990). How we prepare our children for work. In *America's Choice: High Skills or Low Wages*. Rochester, NY: National Center on Education and the Economy.

Cross, K.P. (1981). *Adults as learners*. San Francisco: Jossey-Bass.

Darkenwald, G.G., and Valentine, T. (1985). Factor structure of deterrents to public participation in adult education. *Adult Educational Quarterly* 24 (4): 177-193.

De Geus, A.P. (1988). Planning as learning. *Harvard Business Review*, March-April, 70-74.

Dertouzos, M.L., Lester, R.K., and Solow, R.M. (1989). *Made in America: Regaining the productive edge*. Cambridge, MA: MIT Press.

Dewey, J. (1938). *Education and Experience*. Kappa Delta Pi.

Docking, R. (1990). Skills bank of Australia. Unpublished paper.

Dole, E. (1989). State of the workforce address, 26 October, 1989. Washington, DC.

Domain, B. (1989). *Fortune,* 3 July, 48-62.

Dreyfus, H., and Dreyfus, S. (1986). *Mind over machine.* New York: Free Press.

Dunnette, M. (1988). What we know and don't know about assessment. Keynote address at National Assessment Conference. December. Minneapolis.

Eurich, N.P. (1985). *Corporate classrooms: The learning business.* Princeton: Carnegie Foundation for the Advancement of Teaching.

—. (1990). *The learning industry: Education for adult workers.* Princeton: Carnegie Foundation for the Advancement of Teaching.

Ferman, L.A., Hoyman, M., Curcher-Gershenfeld, J., and Savoie, E.J., eds. (1991). *Joint training programs — A union-management approach to preparing workers for the future.* Ithaca: ILR Press.

Fisher, J.D., Goff, B.A., Nadler, A., and Chinsky, J.M. (1989). Social psychological influences on help seeking and support from peers. In B.H. Gottlieb (ed.) *Marshaling social support: Formats, processes, and effects.* Newbury Park, PA.: Sage.

Fowler, E.M. (1990). Careers: An emphasis on training for the 1990s. *New York Times,* 25 December.

Freire, P. (1989). *Pedagogy of the oppressed.* New York: Continuum.

Fugate, M., and Chapman, R. (1992). Prior learning assessment: results of a nationwide institutional survey. Chicago: CAEL.

Georgenson, D. (1982). The problem of transfer calls for partnership. *Training and Development Journal* 36: 75-78.

Gold, L. (1990). *Campus roadblock: How federal policies make it difficult for adults to go to college.* Washington, DC: Public Policy Advocates.

Goldberg, D. (1990). Hitting the books late. *Education Review, Washington Post,* 18 November.

Goldstein, M. (1981). Issues of public policy affecting adult learning at the postsecondary level. Unpublished paper for the Commission on Higher Education and the Adult Learner, American Council on Education, Washington, DC.

Greenberg, E. (1990). Pathways patterns: A summary of thirteen studies, 1987-1989. Unpublished paper.

Hackman, J.R., and Oldman, G.R. (1980). *Work redesign*. Reading, MA: Addison Wesley.

Johnston, J. (1989). Workplace preparation and retraining for adults. Paper prepared for the national conference on *A More Productive Workforce: Challenge for Postsecondary Education and its Partners*, January 1989.

Johnstone, J.W., and Rivera, R.J. (1965). *Volunteers for Learning*. Chicago: Aldine.

Keeton, M.T. (1991). An alternative vision for metropolitan universities. *Metropolitan Universities* 2 (3): 53-63.

Kernan-Schloss, A. (1989). *Highlights of a conference on a more productive workforce*. Sponsored by the National Governors' Association, College Board, CAEL, and American Council on Education.

Knowles, M. (1978). *The adult learner: A neglected species.* Houston: Gulf.

Kolb, D. (1984). *Experiential learning: Experience as the source of learning and development.* NJ: Prentice-Hall.

Laker, D.R. (1990). Dual dimensionality of training transfer. *Human Resource Development Quarterly* 1 (3): 209-223.

Laur-Ernst, Ute (1990). The development of the vocational education system (FRG) under the special perspective of the 1992 European integration. Keynote paper at National Conference on Assessment and Standards in Vocational Education and Training, Adelaide, South Australia.

Levi, L. (1990). Occupational stress: Spice of life or kiss of death? *American Psychologist* 45 (10): 1142-1145.

Lewin, K. (1951). *Field theory in social sciences.* New York: Harper & Row.

Lindeman, E.C. (1926). *The meaning of adult education.* New York: New Republic.

Lindsey, E., Homes, V., and McCall, M.W., Jr. (1987). Key events in executives' lives. *Technical Report No. 32.* Greensboro, NC: Center for Creative Leadership.

Locke, E.A., and Latham, G.P. (1990). Work motivation and satisfaction: Light at the end of the tunnel. *Psychological Science* 1(4), 240-246.

Long, H.B. (1983). *Adult learning: Research and practice.* New York: Cambridge.

Lynton, E.A. (1992). Continuing professional education: comparative approaches and lessons. In Hunt, E.S. (ed.) *Professional workers as learners.* Washington, DC: Department of Education, Office of Educational Research and Information (Document #065-000-0531-0).

Magaziner, I., and Patimkin, M. (1989). *The silent war: Inside the global and business battles shaping America's future.* New York: Random House.

Merriam, S.B., and Caffarella, R.S. (1991). *Learning in adulthood.* San Francisco: Jossey-Bass.

Miller, J. (1989). International competitiveness — The compelling force for reformation of human resource development in the United States. *A More Productive Workforce: Challenge for Postsecondary Education,* Little Rock, AR. Sponsored by the National Governors' Association, College Board, CAEL, and American Council on Education.

Millis, B.J. (1992). Fulfilling the promise of the seven principles through cooperative learning: An action agenda for the university classroom. *Journal on Excellence in College Teaching* 2: 139-144

Morrison, R.F., and Brantner, T.M. (1992). What enhances or inhibits learning a new job? A basic career issue. *Journal of Applied Psychology,* 77(6), 926-940.

National Commission on Excellence in Education (1983). *A nation at risk: The imperative for educational reform.* Washington, DC: U.S. Department of Education.

Noe, R.A., and Schmitt, N. (1986). The influence of trainee attitudes on training effectiveness: The test of a model. *Personnel Psychology* 39: 497-523.

Office of Educational Research and Information (OERI) (1990). *Racial/ethnic enrollment in higher education: Fall 1978-Fall 1988.* Washington, DC: National Center for Educational Statistics (NCES).

—. (1988). *Trends in minority enrollment in higher education: Fall 1976-Fall 1988.* Washington, DC: National Center for Educational Statistics (NCES).

Office of Technological Assessment of the U.S. Congress (1990). *Worker training: Competing in the new international economy.* Washington, DC.

Office of Work-Based Learning (1992). *Analysis: Public dialogue on voluntary, industry-based skill standards and certification.* Washington, DC: Employment and Training Administration, December.

Parnell, D. (1985). *The neglected majority.* Washington, DC: Community College Press.

Pascarella, E.T., and Terenzini, P.T. (1991). *How college affects students.* San Francisco: Jossey-Bass.

Piaget, J. (1951). *Plays, dreams, and imitation in childhood.* New York: W. W. Norton.

Porter, L.W., and Lawler, E.E. III (1968). *Managerial attitudes and performance.* Homewood, IL: Irwin.

Quality Education for Minorities Project (1990). *Education that works: An action plan for the education of minorities.* Washington, DC: Carnegie Corporation of New York.

Robertson, I., and Downs, S. (1979). Learning and the predictions of performance: Development of trainability testing in the United Kingdom. *Journal of Applied Psychology* 64: 42-50.

Schlossberg, N.K. (1984). *Counseling adults in transition.* New York: Springer.

Senge, P.M. (1990). The leader's new work: Building learning organizations. *Sloan Management Review,* Fall, 7-23.

Sheckley, B.G. (1985). Effects of individual differences on learning projects completed by adults enrolled in community college courses. *Community College Review* 16 (1): 27-37.

—. (1991). *How workers develop professional competence: Results of a pilot study of fifty workers.* Unpublished manuscript, University of Connecticut.

Spille, H. (1989). Beyond the rhetoric: Toward a system of learning and credentialing for adults. *A More Productive Workforce: Challenge for Postsecondary Education,* Little Rock, AR. Sponsored by the National Governors' Association, College Board, CAEL, and American Council on Education.

Sternberg, R.J. (1987) Teaching intelligence: The application of cognitive psychology to the improvement of intellectual skills. In J.B. Baron and R.J. Sternberg (eds.), *Teaching thinking skills: theory and practice.* New York: W.H. Freeman Co. 182-218.

—. (1988). *The triarchic mind: A new theory of human intelligence.* New York: Viking Penguin.

Stewart, T.A. (1992). U.S. productivity: First but fading. *Fortune,* October 19, 54-57.

Sweet, R. (1988). What do developments in the labour market imply for postcompulsory education in Australia? *Australian Journal of Education* 32 (3): 331-356.

Tan, H. (1988). Private sector training in the United States. Paper prepared for Conference on Employer-Sponsored Training, 1-2 December, Alexandria, VA. Sponsored by the Institute on Education and the Economy. Cited in Vaughn, R.J., & Berryman, S.E. (1989). Employer-sponsored training: Current status, future possibilities. *A More Productive Workforce: Challenge for Postsecondary Education,* Little Rock, AR. Sponsored by the National Governors' Association, College Board, CAEL, and American Council on Education.

Tate, P. (1992). *Closing the skills gap: New solutions.* Chicago: CAEL.

Thomas, A.M. (1991). *Beyond education: A new perspective on society's management of learning.* San Francisco: Jossey-Bass.

Tough, A. (1979). *The adult's learning projects: A fresh approach to theory and practice in adult learning.* 2nd ed. Toronto: Ontario Institute for Studies in Education.

U.S. Army Research Institute (1991). *In the Mind's Eye.* Washington, DC.

U.S. Department of Education, National Center for Educational Statistics (October 1992). Key Statistics on the Noncollegiate Sector of Postsecondary Education: 1990.

U.S. Department of Labor, Bureau of Labor Statistics (1987). *Workforce 2000.* Washington, DC: Government Printing Office.

U.S. Department of Labor, Secretary's Commission on Achieving Necessary Skills (SCANS) (1991). *What work requires of schools: A SCANS report for America 2000.* Washington, DC: U.S. Department of Labor.

Veth, J. (1993). *Job search behavior and employment outcomes.* Unpublished Ph.D. qualifying paper. Storrs: University of Connecticut.

Wlodowski, R.J. (1990). *Enhancing adult motivation to learn.* San Francisco: Jossey-Bass.

INDEX

A

ABC Engineering (case study), 15-16, 17
academic credit (*see* credit)
academic freedom, 193
academic studies, need for redesign of, 131, 159, 195
adult education, 65, 91
        (*see also* education: employer-provided; worksites as learning sites)
adult learners (*see* adult students)
adult students, (*see also* learner-workers, worker-learners)
     barriers for, 150-1
     characteristics of, 18-19, 124-5, 129-30, 151, 161, 179
     learning arenas for, 130, 194-5
     numbers of, 79-80, 124-5
advocacy, for workers, 100-101, 146-52 *passim*, 162-5, 186
America Works, 127-8, 148-9, 199
American College Testing (ACT), 109-10
American Council on Education, 79, 133, 135-6, 192
     Center for Adult Learning and Educational Credentials, 135
American Society for Training and Development (ASTD), 109-11
Ameritech Companies, 13
apprenticeship, 63, 64
assessment of learning, 77, 78, 133, 134, 161, 167, 168-9, 192
AT&T, 12, 13, 64
AT&T-CWA-IBEW Alliance, 42
Australia, 136
automation, 3, 6, 7, 36
automotive industry (*see also* EGDPs, industries)
     commitment to worker development, 13
     layoffs, 12-13

B

Baby Bells, 126
basic skills, 67, 74, 110-12
    U.S. Army program, 67
Bell of Pennsylvania, 13, 170
benefits, fringe, 3, 14, (*see also* EGDPs, WSLEs)
    career advising, 92
    dependent care, 90
    education and training, 88-9, 90, 100, 165-6, 191, 197
    government, 89, 90, 96
    health, 94
boundary spanners, 76, 78
Bowes, Lee and Peter Cove, 128
Brock, William, 105
Bush, George, 83
Business Development and Training Center (BDTC), 38-9
businesses, small, 36
    and human resource development, 37-8
    hiring the skills they need, 37
    pilot venture in Chicago, 39
    training options, 37

C

CAEL (Council for Adult and Experiential Learning),
    14, 26, 42, 43, 44, 75, 96, 97, 99, 100, 126, 131, 149, 150, 153, 155, 156, 160, 192, 197
career advising, counseling, planning,
    34, 36, 76, 92, 122, 124-5, 151, 161-2, 169-70
Carnegie Council on Policy Studies in Higher Education, 78
Carnegie Unit, 64
Carnevale, Anthony P., 63, 111
certificates, 134, 167
certification, 186 (*see also* credentialing)
Chaparral Steel, 185
Chicago, 39
child care, 90, 94, 158, 165
classroom
    programs, role of, 177-9
    training, limitations of, 181-2
classroom learning,
    challenged by worksites, 173
    transfer to workplace, 27-8, 174, 181
coalitions (*see* partnerships, EGDPs, WSLEs)
collective bargaining, 13-14, 25, 34-5
colleges and universities, 61-81 *passim*, 119-39 *passim*

as partners in employability programs, 61, 68, 80, 99
benefits from participation in employability programs, 62, 75, 79-81
contributions to worker employability, 55, 68-9, 100
corporate, 63
curricular and content changes needed, 71, 159, 195
experience with adult students, 73, 79-80
flexibility, 71, 77
institutional barriers, 69-75, 166-8
new roles for, 68-9
public policy for, 191
public subsidies for, 94
range of services, 73-4, 76-9
requirements for successful participation in employability programs,
    62, 75-9
resistance to change, 78-9
slow response time of, 70, 72
teaching methods, 71
College Board, 79
college students, age of, 79-80, 124-5
Commission on the Skills of the American Workforce, 67, 109-10, 122, 143
Communications Workers of America (CWA), 13, 59, 64, 170, 172
community college/s, 33, 64, 65, 74, 75
competence, a continuum of, 179-81
competencies (*see* skills)
competition, competitiveness, 5-7, chapter 2 *passim*, 193
    among education providers, 61, 192
    and employability, 20-21
    causes of failure in, 12
    effect on of disadvantages workers, 146
    global, 13, 20
    Japanese, 16
    old style, 14-16
    strategy for achieving, 5-8, 11, 30, throughout text *passim*
competitive situation of disadvantages, 104
competitive strategy of Third World countries, 105
competitors, 83
Connecticut, Department of Labor, 97
continual learning cycle, 183-5
continuous improvement (*see also* TQM)
    Fortune 500 companies, 16-17
cooperative education, 122-3
corporate colleges, 63
Council for Adult and Experiential Learning (*see* CAEL)
counseling (*see* career advising, counseling, planning)
credentialing,
    alternative system needed, 20-21, 93, 103, 132-9, 192
    proposed national system, 135-6

credit(s), academic, 134, 192
customer(s), 6-7

D

deficit, 83
deGeus, Arie, 16
degrees, 134
deskilled, deskilling, 6, 7, 15, 40, 58, 105
disadvantaged workers, attitudes toward, 141-52 *passim* (*see also* workers)
disincentives to employability, 88-91,
    (*see also* incentives to employability, 92-5)
    adult education, lack of information on, 91
    dependent care, 90 (*see also* child care)
    employee education benefits, taxation of, 90-1
    food stamps, 90
    institutional barriers, 69-75, 166-8
    job training partnership act, administration of, 91
    student financial assistance, 88-9
    unemployment insurance, 89
    vocational rehabilitation, 90
    vocational-technical education, 91
    welfare, 89
divestiture, 12
drop-out rate, 121
Dusco Community Services (DCS), 40-42, 123-4, 149

E

economies,
    Eastern European, 88
    fair play in, 88
economy
    functioning, 99, 189
    global (world), 6, chapter 2 *passim*, 87
    unsolved problems, 119
education (*see also* training)
    costs, 94, 196-7
    employer provided, 18, 148, 155-71 *passim*
    European views on integration of systems, 9
        new patterns of, 18
    financing, 189
    future needs, 184
    government's role in, 11
    new strategy for, 17-20, 189, 191
    non-system, 9, 192

planning (individual), 26, 124 (*see also* career advising)
prior, as precondition for future training, 142-4
providers, diversity of, 9, 61-6, 93
role in employability programs, 61-81
saves employer costs, 40
return to, 18, 19
skills training for lower paid workers, 40-42
transfer to worksite, 27-8, 196
two systems, 25, 27-8, 30
value of, 5, 8-9, 14, 141
educational benefits, 33, 90 (*see also* tuition aid)
educational institutions
(*see* colleges and universities, community colleges, schools, vocational/technical schools)
employability
benefits of for states, 84-5
building blocks of a nationwide program, 98-101
changes that must occur, 189-90
continual learning cycle for, 183-5
curriculum, 109-13
defined, 4-5, 49, 105, 194-5
discrepancies in opportunities for achieving, 141-4
education for, 25-30
education/training system as barrier to, 20-21
emphasis on, 13
financing national program, 196-9
framework for, 20, 21
gap, 141
goal of 95%, 5, 10
government disincentives to, 88-91
government incentives for, 92-5
opportunity for, 13
partnerships required, 6, 7, 8-9, 185-7, 190 (*see also* partnerships)
philanthropic role in, 200
policies that hinder, 88-91
practical option for U.S., 5
programs (*see* employee growth and development programs)
retraining required, 10
skills needed (*see* skills, requirements for work)
toward a national policy, 189-202
universal, 30, 88, 189-90, 190-3, 194, 202
ways to sustain, 7, 10, 84, 146-7, 173
employability skills as cognitive processing, 115-18
EGDPs (*see* employee growth and development programs)
employee growth and development programs, 13, 25-27, 61, 132, 197
access, 163, 185

advocacy for by partners, 162-3
as investments, 36
automotive and telecommunications companies involvement in,
13-14, 25-27, 36, 126
benefits of participation in,
for employers, 31-36, 39-40, 48
for schools, 62, 75, 79-80, 196
for unions, 33-4, 57-60
for workers, 33-4, 49-53, 196
broker-manager services, 171
choice for worker-learners, 156-7
components of, 26, 44, 51-2, 126, 139, 151, 155-72
costs of participation in,
for employers, 33, 34, 42-4, 48, 100
for government, 198-9
for schools, 75-9
for unions, 57-8
for workers, 36, 50, 54-5, 158
counseling and support services, 151, 162, 169-70
employers' roles in, 26-7, 194-5
funding for, 14, 131-2
individual employee's responsibility, 27
goals and values, 170-1
obstacles to, 95
outreach, 163-5
participation in, 26, 42-3, 150-1, 156, 164-5, 166
prepaid tuition, 165-6
principles of, 155-72
prior learning assessment (PLA), 165, 167, 168-9
proactive outreach, 163-5
removing institutional barriers, 166-8
research and technical services for, 101
Returning to Learning® Workshop, 35, 70, 160-1, 165
role of CAEL in, 26, 99, 100, 130, 171
role of classroom programs in, 177-9
success of, 126
support for, 60
public policy, 101
unions' role in, 27, 49, 57-9
workplace support systems, 169-70
employee/s (*see also* worker/s)
education benefits, 90, 100
training tax, 93
employers
(*see also* EGDPs, benefits of participation in; costs of participation in)
as partners in employability programs, 31-48

as sponsors of training, 148
worker skills preferences, 68
employment security, 141 (*see also* employability, job security)
enterprises, high performance
experiential learning, 77, 132, 168, 178-87 *passim*

F

federal and state governments
    actions to take, 92, 198-9
    as partners, 83-101
    employability programs sponsored by, 96
    how they benefit from employability, 84, 86
    policies that hinder employability, 88-91, 95
    policies that support, 101, 149-50, 198-9
    ways they can act, 83-4, 92-4, 95, 146-7, 198-9, 201
Federal Reserve Board, 201
Federal Second-Chance Programs, 64
Federal Trade Commission, 192
financial aid for education, 77, 100, 146, 165-6, 199 (*see also* benefits)
Ford Motor Company, 14, 26-7, 53
Fortune 500 companies, 16, 100, 130, 200
Fox, Larry, 58
France, 93

G

Gebhart, Richard, 67
gender, differences in training opportunities by, 142
General Educational Development (GED), 64, 65
General Electric, 16-17
generic skills, 68
Georgia, 96, 170
German vocational system, 68, 109-10
Germany, 11, 12, 30, 105, 130
Great Valley Corporate Center, 38
government, (*see also* federal and state)
    how it helps employability programs, 86, 92-7, 192
    how it hinders employability programs, 86, 88-91, 190, 191
    incentives, 149-50
    new roles for, 20-21
    responsibility for education, training, 11
governors, efforts toward employability, 84, 193
Governor's Summit on Workforce Development, 96

H

Hatfield, Mark, 67
Head Start, 124
health benefits, 94
health, poor, 95
high performance
    achievement of, 182-5
    enterprises, 5-8
    work cycles, 173, 184-5
    work organizations, 7, 189
    work settings, 184
high skills, high pay, 7
higher education
    (*see* colleges and universities, community colleges, vocational/
    technical institutes and education)
human capital, investment in, 12
human resource development, 195-6
    effective systems, 30
    lack of policy, 20, 190
    role of formal school in, 20
    undervaluation of, 45

I

illiteracy, 9, 19-20, 141, 158
incentives to employability, 189
    for employed workers, 92-4
    for unemployed workers, 94-5
Indiana, 96, 170
industries (*see also* EGDPs, WSLEs)
    automotive, 12-13, 25, 36, 170
    candy making, 26
    construction, 26
    electronics, 87
    food service, 33-4, 41
    paper manufacturing, 26, 32-3, 164
    retailing, 34, 41, 149
    steel, 12, 96, 185
    telecommunications, 12, 13, 26, 36
    textiles, 87
infrastructure for employability, 8, 9, 10, 20-1, 98
International Brotherhood of Electrical Workers (IBEW), 13, 59, 170, 172

J

Japan, 11, 12, 16, 29-30, 105, 130
job growth, 10
job loss, 3, 4, 10
job security, 5, 11 (*see also* employment security)
    diminished, 12
    obsolete, 13
job search skills, 138-9
job seeking, responsibility for, 5-6
job skill requirements, 10, 19-20
Job Training Partnership Act, 91
jobs, development of skills on, 173-5
Jobs for the Future, 101
John, Jules, and Joan (fictional characters), 3-4, 5-6, 7, 8, 56-7, 155, 184-5
joint ventures teams, 131
joint ventures,
    labor and management, 13-14, 26
Joyce Foundation, 96

K

kaizen, 16
Kearns, David, 142
Kellogg Foundation, W.K., 96
Kennedy, Edward, 67
knowledge, rapid growth of, 19
knowledge requirements for work, 19
    (*see also* qualifications workers need, skills requirements)

L

labor/management sponsored training, 13-14
Language, as indicator of training opportunity, 144
Laur-Ernst, Ute, 109
layoffs, 3, 5, 10
leadership
    proactive, chapter 13
learners, adults as, 18 (*see also* adult students)
    increasing numbers of, 18
learner-workers (*see also* adult students, worker-learners)
    as partners in employability programs, 158
    attitudes towards education, 159
    choices, 156-7
    contributions to employability programs, 158
    information they need, 159-62
    profiles of, 158-9

learning
    application to problems and issues in workplace, 195
    collaboration or team, 175
    continual cycle of, 183
    efficiency, 195
    environments, 173
    in the workplace, 11, 55-7, 173-87 (*see also* WSLEs)
    internalized barriers to, 95
    lifelong, 79, 106-7, 132, 184
    need for change in, 18 (*see also* WSLEs)
    organizations, 46-8, 61, 173-87 *passim*
    organizations and total quality management, 46-8
    strategy, 17
    system, 30, 61, 63, 132, 191
    teams, 29
legislation, 83-101 *passim*
literacy of workers, 9, 40 (*see also* illiteracy)

M

managers (*see* supervisors)
Marshall, Ray, 105
Massachusetts Institute of Technology, 16, 143
    Quality Education for Minorities Project, 146
Mazda, 16
mental self-management, 115-18
Mill, John Stuart, 59
Miller, Jerry, 20
MIT Commission on Productivity, 29, 44-5
Mountain Bell/CWA/IBEW PATHWAYS to the Future, 166

N

Nation at Risk, A, 119-20
National Center for Educational Statistics (NCES), 79
National Center on Education and the Economy (NCEE), 6
National Development and Training Center of UAW/Ford, 126
National Employability Council (proposed), 201-2
National Football League (NFL), 87-8
national performance standards, 67
New York, 96, 170
"nickel fund", 14
non-collegiate vocational schools, 64
non-traditional students (*see* adult students)

O

Ohio, 96, 97, 170

P

paid educational leave, 93
Parnell, Dale, 124
partners (*see also* partnerships)
    corporations as, 31-48, 100
    education providers as, 61-80, 99
    federal and state governments as, 83-101
    workers and unions as, 49-60
partnerships for employability, 7, 8-9, 19, 30, 61, 150, 185-7, 190, 191, 200-2
    how they can work, chapters 3 to 7
    intra-state, 93
    roles of, 185-7
pensions, 3
performance standards, 91
Perkins Ace of 1984, 89, 91
philanthropies, 200
policy, public for national employability, 191-3, 196-9
political power decentralized, 11
PONSI, 133
postsecondary education, 89
prepaid tuition (*see* assessment of learning)
prior experience in a new job, 174
prior learning assessment (PLA), 77, 78, 133, 134, 161, 167, 168-9, 192
productivity, 6, 29, 84
    and educational qualifications, 195
    comparison of Japanese and American workers, 29-39
    MIT Commission on, 29-30, 44-45
    of American worker, 115
profitability, 12

Q

QED Engineering (case study), 28-9, 46
qualifications workers need, 103

R

race,
    differences in training opportunities by, 142
    percent in workforce, 145
Regula, Ralph, 67
relocation of workers, 26

retail training, 40-42
Returning to Learning® Workshop, 52, 160-2, 165

S

school-to-work transition, 67
schools, (*see also* colleges and universities, community colleges, vocational/technical institutes)
 adopt-a-school programs, 67
 as partners in employability programs, 61-80
 basic skills training in, 66-7
 benefits from participating in employability programs, 62
 client-centered orientation, 148
 inadequate performance of, 9, 66-7
 public policy for, 191
 public, role of, 63, 66-8
 requirements for participation in employability programs, 75-8
 variety of, 63-4
Scott Paper Company, 170
Senge, Peter, 16
Shell Corporation, 16
skills bank, 136 (*see also* credentialing)
skills credentialing, benefits to, 136-8
 all partners, 138
 educators and human resource managers, 137-8
 employees, 136-7
 employers, 137
 industries, 137
 national, state, and local governments, 138
 unions, 137
skills deficiencies, 105, 106, 119
skills development on job, 173-9
skills gap, closing the, 103, chapter 8, 119-139
 costs to workers, 130-31
 scale of effort, 130
skills, novice to expert continuum, 179-81
skills requirements for work, 5, 66, 105-18, 157
 ability to learn, 108, 110-11, 184
 communication skills, 106, 107, 110-12, 184
 cognitive, intellectual, 110-12, 115-18, 123, 184
 computational, 19, 107, 110-12
 consensus on, 109-10
 flexibility, adaptability, 106, 110, 184
 generic, 68, 107, 114, 157
 information processing, 20
 interpersonal, 40, 110-11, 113

     job specific, 196
     leadership, 110, 113
     organizational effectiveness, 110, 113
     personal and career development, 110, 112-13
     problem solving, 108, 110-12
     professional and technical, 108, 114
     reading, 19, 40, 110-12
     specific vs. generic, 108
     systems thinking, 110, 111
     teamwork or group skills, 106, 108, 110, 113, 184
skills, standards, 136
skills, what employees think they need, 108-9
skills, transferable, transferability, 114-15, 125, 131
small businesses, 26, 37-9, 100, 172, 201
Spille, Henry A., 135
state programs of employees growth and development, 84, 85
states as partners for employability, 83-101
states, potential for leadership, 96-7
Sternberg, R.J., 115-18
student financial assistance, 88-9
     Perkins or Stafford loans, 89
supervisors,
     as instructors, 175-7
     learning expectations set by, 174-5
     role in training, 175-7
Sweden, 93

T

tax credits for employers, 92
tax incentives for employees, 90, 91
taxes, 197, 199
Taylor, Taylorism, Taylorist, 7, 122
technology, effect of, 12, 19, 26-27
Tennessee Valley Authority, 201
total quality management (TQM), 16, 46-8, 175-6
     (*see also* continuous improvement)
     and training, 46-8
TQM (*see* total quality management)
TRAC/USA©, 40-42, 123-4, 149
training,
     as a business strategy, 44-6, 173-87
     attitudes toward, 45
     corporate, 63, 191-2, 194
     cost of, 34, 63, 195-6
     designed on novice to expert continuum, 181

in-house, 197
  state subsidies for, 93, 94
  transfer of to work setting, 178, 196
  who receives it, 142-4, 163
transferability of workplace skills, 114-15
transitions, 119-29
  adaptation to, 120
  college to work, 120, 124-5
  high school to work, 120, 121-4
  management of, 121
  welfare to school and work, 120, 127-8
  work to school, 120, 125-6
tuition aid, assistance, 34, 156, 165-6
  average use of, 130, 166
  employer provided, 92
  prepaid, 165-6
  taxed as current income, 92
two-tiered society, avoiding, 141-52 *passim*

U

unemployed workers, incentives for, 94-5
  underestimating potential of, 95
unemployment,
  cost of, 3-4, 95, 194
  insurance, 89
  structural, 85
United Auto Workers (UAW), 14, 170
United Food and Commercial Workers (UFCW), 170
UAW-Ford, 42-3, 64, 126
  CUOP (College and University Options Program), 53, 59, 160
  National Training and Development Center, 59, 172
unions, (*see also* employee growth and development programs)
  as advocates of employability programs, 58-9, 186
  as learning resources, 192
  as partners in employability programs, 49, 57-60, 200
U.S. Department of Agriculture, 96, 170
U.S. Department of Education, 79
U.S. Department of Labor, 13, 170
U.S. Secretary of Labor's Commission on Achieving Necessary Skills
(SCANS), 109-10, 181
University of Connecticut, 97
  Research Center for Organizational Learning, 28
US WEST Communications, 13, 64, 170, 172

V

vocational preparation, lack of, 66-7
vocational/technical institutes and education,
        63, 64, 65, 68, 74, 91, 105-6, 121-2

W

welfare, 85, 89, 94, 127-8, 149, 150
Wisconsin Bell, 170
work,
        as school, 128-9
        ethic, 29, 107, 112-13, 123
        experience as indicator of training opportunity, 144
worker/s,
        as partners in employability programs, 49-55
        benefits of employability programs for, 49, 50, 186-7
        benefits of highly qualified, 85
        disadvantaged, 145-6, 150, 150-2
        employed, incentives for, 92-3
        -learner/s, 150-1, 156-62 (*see also* adult students, learner-workers)
        individually chosen learning, 157, 194
        multiple roles of, 150
        overcoming pattern of disadvantage, 146-7, 148-52
        potential to develop skills, 105
        responsibility for developing skills, 191, 198
        retirement, 196
        unemployed, incentives for, 94-5
        untrained and unskilled, 106, 145-6
workforce,
        development, 199, 200, (*passim* throughout text)
        globally competitive, 99, 189
        in year 2000, 19, 145
        literacy rates, 19
        qualified, 19
        skills needed, 19-20
        U.S., 99, 194
workplace opportunities, taking advantage of, 56-7
worksettings as learning environments (WSLEs),
        25, 27-30, 55-7, 128, 173-87 *passim*, 189, 194
        achieving high performance in, 182-5
        characteristics of, 176-7
        continuum of competence in, 179-81
        developing skills on job, 173-5
        limitations of classroom training in, 181-2
        partnerships roles in, 185-7
        requirements for, 185-8

role of classroom programs in, 177-9
supervisors as instructors in, 174-7
workers benefit from, 186-7
World War II, 9, 11
WSLEs (*see* worksettings as learning environments)

ABOUT THE AUTHORS

BARRY G. SHECKLEY,

Associate Professor of Education and Director of the Research Project for Organizational Learning at the University of Connecticut, consults with numerous multi-national corporations in areas vital to improving productivity, such as computer-integrated manufacturing, project management, corporate training programs, management assessment centers, total quality manufacturing, and time-based management. His focused consulting experiences with business enterprises has provided Sheckley with years of experience in developing innovative perspectives on developing the employability skills of American workers. The strategies Sheckley outlines are based on his extensive research on the adult learning process. His numerous articles on topics from the self-directed nature of adult learning to adult learning as a recursive process are published both domestically and internationally. Sheckley's experience includes roles as dean of a community college, associate director of a university research center, and director of five National Institutes on Adult and Experiential Learning for CAEL. He received his doctorate at the University of Connecticut.

LOIS LAMDIN,

business consultant and author, has many years of day-to-day experience working with senior executives and their employees to provide education and training directly relevant to the specific needs of the business and the individual. Lamdin has also worked with CAEL in developing its joint ventures programs, gaining expertise in building collaborative relationships with corporations, unions, education institutions, and state and national government agencies. Most recently Lamdin has worked to design and implement a school-to-work program in retailing based at major shopping malls in four states. She also publishes and writes a column for the *Great Valley Business News* and has done extensive consulting and writing on joint ventures, serving adult learners, and assessing prior learning. Her academic experience includes teaching literature at Carnegie-Mellon, serving as associate dean at Empire State College, and directing a consortium of 34 colleges in southeastern Pennsylvania. Lamdin received her doctorate at the University of Pittsburgh.

MORRIS T. KEETON

is Director of the Institute for Research on Adults in Higher Education at University of Maryland University College. He is President Emeritus of CAEL and Senior Consultant to the President and Trustees of Cambridge College. Keeton has served on the faculty of the Institute for the Management of Lifelong Education, Harvard Graduate School of Education, and later served on its advisory board. Among numerous positions he has held in the past, Keeton was President of the American Association for Higher Education, Chair of the American Council on Education's Commission on Higher Education and the Adult Learner, and served on the executive board of the North Central Association of Colleges and Schools, Commission on Institutions of Higher Education. Keeton served on the faculty of Antioch College for 30 years, and was its chief academic officer for 14 of those years. Keeton has written extensively. His primary writings deal with ethical theory, theory of knowledge, college and university governance, experiential learning, and adult learning at the postsecondary level. Keeton received his doctorate from Harvard University and has since received eight honorary doctorates.

3_21

FIGURE LIST

Figure 4.1 How Employers Benefit from
Employability Programs
Situation 1: Declining Productivity of Aging
Workforce, Competition Forcing Higher
Productivity per Worker 32

Figure 4.2 How Employers Benefit from
Employability Programs
Situation 2: Rapid Turnover of Entry-level
Employees 34

Figure 4.3 How Employers Benefit from
Employability Programs
Situation 3: Need for Downsizing to Allow
Technology-based Gains in Efficiency &
Enable Starts on New Subsidiary Enterprises;
Unionized, Bargaining Triennially 35

Figure 4.4 How Employers Benefit from
Employability Programs
Situation 4: Small Business with Minimal
Funds for Employee Development 37

Figure 5.1 How Workers Benefit from Employability
Programs 50

Figure 6.1 How Education Providers Benefit from
Employability Programs...62

Figure 6.2 Matrix of Providers..64

Figure 6.3 Why Corporations Don't Turn to Colleges for
Their Training Needs..70

Figure 6.4   Requirements for Schools' Participation in
Employability Programs...78

Figure 7.1   How Governments Help & Benefit in
Employability Programs...86

Figure 8.1   Skills Needed by the American Workforce............110

Figure 11.1   What Broker-Managers of Employability
Programs Do..171

Figure 12.1   Transfer of Training in Two Different
Work Settings...178

Figure 12.2   The Continuum of Competence..............................180

Figure 12.3   Continual Learning Cycle for Lifelong
Employability..183